Growing Up i

D1518011

SOCIAL
DEVELOPMENT
OF THREE- AND
FOUR-YEAR-OLDS

Susan A. Miller, EdD

Gryphon House
www.gryphonhouse.com

Published by Gryphon House, Inc.
P. O. Box 10, Lewisville, NC 27023
800.638.0928; 877.638.7576 (fax)
Visit us on the web at www.gryphonhouse.com.

Bulk Purchase
Gryphon House books are available for special premiums and sales promotions as well as for fund-raising use. Special editions or book excerpts also can be created to specifications. For details, call 800.638.0928.

Disclaimer
Gryphon House, Inc., cannot be held responsible for damage, mishap, or injury incurred during the use of or because of activities in this book. Appropriate and reasonable caution and adult supervision of children involved in activities and corresponding to the age and capability of each child involved are recommended at all times. Do not leave children unattended at any time. Observe safety and caution at all times.

Library of Congress Cataloging-in-Publication Data
The Cataloging-in-Publication Data is registered with the Library of Congress for ISBN 978-0-87659-663-0.

DEDICATION

For Adam, my serious, yet ever-so-smart and curious grandson, who allowed me to share many of these wonderfully insightful illustrations about his childhood.

PRAISE FOR SUSAN A. MILLER'S BOOKS IN THE GROWING UP IN STAGES SERIES

SHARON MACDONALD,
author and educator

Susan has been a personal friend and a resource for me since my classroom days teaching four-year-olds in San Antonio, Texas, and on through my years on the road speaking to teachers about the ages and stages of early childhood development. I always sought out her opinions and insights. Now I do not have to call her. I have her books!

Her understanding of social, cognitive, and emotional development in young children is unrivaled. She explains ages and stages in her unique way—clean, simple, honest. She is a gifted writer with real empathy and understanding for her subjects—children.

Susan Miller's books belong in the personal library of any early childhood teacher. Buy them.

DEBBIE VERA
PhD, associate professor and chair of the Department of Educator and Leadership Preparation, Texas A&M University

While reading the scenarios, I could easily see how all three domains in this series—emotional, social, and cognitive development—are interdependent. This series provides a holistic view of the child and really helps the reader to understand the overlap of development into each domain.

The writing style is personal and engaging for teachers.

CONTENTS

Acknowledgments. vi

Introduction 1

1. Forming Friendships 6

2. Learning to Share and Cooperate 13

3. Creating Happiness. 19

4. Dealing with Teasing. 26

5. Participating in Rough-and-Tumble Play. 32

6. Exploring Diversity 39

7. Developing Gender Awareness 45

8. Developing Active Listening Skills. 52

9. Building Verbal Communication Skills. 59

10. Participating in Imaginative Play. 66

11. Milestones in Social Development 73

Index. 76

ACKNOWLEDGMENTS

My family—Peter, Gregg, Owen, and Adam—for their support and patience.

My typist of many years, Karen Epting, for her professionalism and sense of humor.

Librarian Julie Daigle, for her invaluable assistance with researching children's books.

Diane Ohanesian, for encouraging me to write this series.

Gryphon House staff members Stephanie Roselli, for answering my many questions; Terrey Hatcher, for her thorough and very thoughtful editing; and Anna Wilmoth, for her assistance with details and publicity.

INTRODUCTION

Over the years, since I was a child-development student at Syracuse University, I have so often thought of the sound advice given by a very wise professor, Elizabeth Manwell. She explained the importance of observing young children in their daily surroundings. Through observation, you can become aware of children's social interactions with each other. By observing carefully, you tune into how young children use materials and solve problems. By assessing a series of written observations, a teacher can see patterns of development: Is a child struggling? Taking a leadership role? Dependent on adults?

As college students, we discussed our observations out in the field. Soon we discovered pertinent connections between understanding various stages of child development and planning relevant curriculum and appropriate teaching strategies, as well as monitoring a child's progress. The importance of observation and applying an understanding of the stages of child development principles as the basis for appropriate teaching practices has been my guide for forty years.

In another situation, Dr. Manwell used a line from Rogers and Hammerstein's musical *South Pacific* as a topic for a parent workshop: "You've got to be carefully taught . . . to hate all the people your relatives hate." This powerful social message from the 1960s still rings true today. I have never forgotten the dynamic discussions that took place in a racially troubled community during that evening workshop, which included African American and white families, preschool teachers, and Dr. Manwell. The response from the audience was clear—we must begin with our young children. They need to learn to live and play together in socially positive ways. It is up to the adults in their lives (parents and teachers) to support them so this will happen. We need to remember to practice this concept every day in our work with children.

What You Will Notice

By their nature, preschoolers are social beings. They find it easy to make friends spontaneously. Typically, three-year-olds have various friends for different activities. Interested in playing with their peers, they shift from parallel play to developing ways to interact with their friends. Becoming more socially competent, four-year-olds find it fun to enter into collaborative activities with several friends as they discuss and acknowledge each other's ideas. Many four-year-olds enter into best-friend relationships and enjoy telling secret silly jokes, wearing matching outfits, and sharing special rituals.

Playing together involves sharing, but that is certainly a difficult concept for egocentric three-year-olds to understand. It is confusing for them to comprehend why they don't necessarily have to share a personal possession, but they need to share a school toy, even when they had it first! However, when three-year-olds do not have a vested interest in materials, they discover it can be fun to share and play cooperatively. Less egocentric, four-year-olds are delighted to enter into self-initiated cooperative efforts where they find it is exciting to share all kinds of things, such as their ideas, friends' company, art materials, and their feelings.

Preschoolers are happiest when they have plenty of time for involvement in unstructured play. Although three-year-olds find great pleasure in connecting with their favorite adults, four-year-olds are ever so happy expanding their social relationships by interacting with their friends, especially their best friends.

While preschoolers are interacting with classmates and playing with friends, they often begin experimenting with teasing. Teasing is a form of play that can be fun when both parties are enjoying themselves. However, three-year-olds are frequently not successful in their teasing because they are not sophisticated enough to know what makes something funny or to understand how the other person feels. Sometimes, four-year-olds think teasing with bathroom words and shocking others is funny. However, when they try to gain attention by teasing, the result can be annoyance. Not all teasing is verbal, such as when preschoolers poke each other, play tickling games, or chase one another.

During rough-and-tumble play, three- and four-year-olds seem to instinctively tune into their own movements and those of others, as they learn to read body language. Rough-and-tumble play provides opportunities for preschoolers to try out leader and follower roles as they learn to develop a sense of fairness. Socially, they become aware of what their playmates like or do not like and learn to adjust their play accordingly.

By three, as soon as preschool children are comfortably able to label themselves as a boy or a girl, they demonstrate a preference for gender-typed play activities. Most four-year-olds prefer playing with friends of the same sex—just check out all of the boys in the block area! Preschoolers focus on gender cues they have received from those around them as well as from media and technology, and stereotypical mixed messages frequently encourage them to react with negative behaviors, such as excluding the opposite sex from activities.

Somewhere between the ages of three and five, preschoolers become aware of racial categories, although they do not always classify themselves accurately. Around age four-and-a-half, many preschoolers decenter and become less egocentric, which enables them to piece together their own identities and explore how they are similar to or diverse from others. Celebrating family, national, and religious holidays is a wonderful way for three- and four-year-olds to learn in natural ways from their peers and teachers about their diverse cultures.

As they develop an ear for different sounds, three-year-olds find it fun to listen to and repeat nursery rhymes, songs, and finger plays. Besides listening to each other's preposterously silly banter throughout the day, four-year-olds love to listen to funny jokes and riddles—even if they don't understand them! Dialogues may become rather lengthy as they begin to understand the importance of using their receptive powers to obtain information.

An important step toward learning to interact with others occurs when preschoolers use their expressive verbal language skills to share their ideas, needs, and feelings. Through books, three- and four-year-olds are introduced to a vast technical vocabulary, which helps them understand words in context and associate an activity with a group of words. Three-year-olds enjoy retelling stories and can recall key events in order. Adding props to preschoolers' dramatic play can help enhance and build their communication skills.

During imaginative play, three-year-olds are not quite sure whether things are make-believe or real. However, even though four-year-old play can be filled with fantasy, they have a good sense of what is fantasy or reality. Three-year-olds' imitative imaginative play themes are built around experiences with friends and family life; later in development, four-year-olds expand their pretend ideas to include the community. Frequently, four-year-olds are motivated in their imaginative play by wild superheroes or villains. However, if they are encouraged to develop their own imaginative dialogues and make good choices, they may turn out to be powerful rescuers and save the world!

By understanding more about these areas of social development and exploring the related strategies suggested in this book, you can encourage appropriate interactions and celebrate the growth of preschoolers in your care.

As You Read This Book

As you start each chapter, you will find a definition for the chapter's theme. As you read on, you may wish to think about and add your own definition on a sticky note.

Next are some highlights of developmental milestones of three- and four-year-olds. These will help you understand the stage of social development that a preschooler is functioning in during a specific time.

Then I will share some scenarios related to the chapter topic. These snapshot views are taken from events that happened with the children in my various classrooms (names changed, of course), from observations that I have been fortunate enough to make in preschool programs around the United States and abroad, and from special memories of my grandsons at particular three- and four-year-old stages. Related to the different scenarios are explanations of the stages to help you understand why a behavior or action is or is not occurring at that specific time. As we are all aware, individual preschool children may develop at different rates—some a little slowly, and others more rapidly.

Although I would like very much to have a face-to-face conversation with each reader, that of course is not possible. So what I have tried to do, as the author and a teacher, is to write in a conversational tone discussing the stages that young children go through. Rather than burdening you with heavy research and theoretical references, I have attempted to keep the flow of observation and application light and practical.

Next you will discover guidance specifically for you, the teacher or caregiver. The section called What You Can Do is designed to serve as a springboard by providing exciting curriculum activities or helpful teaching strategies for you to try with the children in your care. Feel free to build on these ideas and write on sticky notes to make this section your own.

The Other Aspects to Consider—Alerts section deals with circumstances that you might have questions about, such as when children are not quite in step with the social-development milestones for their age. This may indicate that you or a child's parents should consider seeking professional assistance for answers.

The ideas in the Activities for Parents to Try at Home portion are fun, easy-to-accomplish adventures appropriate for parents to explore with their children. You may wish to share these ideas with parents during conferences, online, in your newsletter, or by posting on a bulletin board. If you like, ask parents to share their own ideas on the topic and to provide photos of the activities for everyone to enjoy afterward.

Finally, a special section suggests fascinating books to read with children. All of the literature is related to the chapter topic and just begs you and the children to look at the enticing pictures, talk about the words, and enter into a dialogue about what is happening on the pages. Research shows that reading to young children is the most important way to stimulate their desire to become readers.

As you read this book, I hope you enjoy your adventures observing young children and learning how various social-development milestones affect the different stages of the lives of three- and four-year-olds.

1

FORMING **FRIENDSHIPS**

Friendship—a mutual-affection relationship among individuals who may have similar interests

et's take a glimpse into what you might observe as three- and four-year-olds grow socially. Although not all children develop at the same rate or achieve specific milestones at the same time, you can probably expect to see some of the following behaviors as friendships evolve among the preschoolers in your care:

- Three-year-olds make friends spontaneously.
- Three-year-olds often select friends because of their proximity.
- Three-year-olds have become interested in playing with their peers.
- Four-year-olds discuss and acknowledge each other's ideas.
- Four-year-olds may become frustrated if one friend always dominates the play.
- Four-year-olds show a preference for same-sex best friends.

Now, let's look at some scenarios of how children in your classroom might be interacting with playmates and developing friendships.

At school, three-year-old Tom enjoys building towers using Lego bricks with his friend Paul. When Tom goes outside, he likes to fill up the red wagon with leaves with his buddy

Jeb. Then, when Tom and his mom walk home from school together, they stop in the park, where he has great fun creating a huge mound of sand with his park friend, Michael.

Friendships for three-year-olds are often spontaneous and fluid. The child's playmate at that moment is most likely to be called his friend. He has various friends for different activities. Not needing any introductions, three-year-olds easily move in and out of play with new friends when their interests change. This type of play offers three-year-olds a chance to hone their social skills and develop their language abilities as they converse with their friends. They are sharpening their problem-solving skills while learning how to form and dissolve their attachments to others.

Because their friends are apt to change when their activities and interests change, three-year-olds, like Tom, might refer to a specific friend as a "park friend" or a "Lego buddy." Often, they select friends because they are nearby at the time, playing with an interesting toy, or par-ticipating in a fun activity. A three-year-old may actually be more inter-ested in the toy than the other child. Sometimes, an exciting skill, such as building a high pile of leaves, might be the attraction. At other times, a three-year-old might admire a  friend's particular physical attribute, such as having a lovely long ponytail, or an exceptional strength, such as being able to carry a stack of three big, hollow wooden blocks at one time.

Although young three-year-olds still enjoy their parents' or teacher's attention while playing, they are quite interested in playing with their peers too. Socially, they are shifting from sitting right next to their friend in parallel play to learning how to interact with others. For example, as Tom's Lego friend, Paul, stacks one block on top of the next, Tom imitates this action. This imitative form of play lets Paul know, "I really like your actions and I think you are a cool friend!" This interaction might encourage the two children to have a con-versation or play together with their manipulative materials.

Still rather egocentric, three-year-olds may have ideas about friendship that are quite self-centered. For example, it is difficult for three-year-olds to share. If a competition arises between two friends for a particular object that both children desire, this may weaken the new friendship and cause one child to move on and look for a more interesting playmate or activity. Or one play friend might grab the desirable item and claim it for himself, which could also hamper the friendship.

With better communication skills and their emerging social competence, four-year-olds are more apt to see a situation from another child's perspective. They are more cooperative and find it exciting and fun to participate in collaborative activities. For this reason, they love small-group projects. For example, when several boys discover some empty cardboard boxes, they enthusiastically put their heads together in shared planning. The four-year-olds discuss and acknowledge each other's ideas. Then they decide on Anselm's suggestion to make a rocket ship. Because four-year-olds enjoy having a friend's approval, Doug says to Anselm, "I'll get tape to stick boxes together. OK?"

Although four-year-olds can have several close friends, sometimes the addition of an extra child to a project makes it uncomfortable for the original little group of friends. Fortunately, older four-year-olds are learning how to use their negotiation skills. For instance, Teddy offers to trade a special can of booster rocket fuel if Anselm and Doug will let him ride on their rocket. As part of the social learning process, four-year-olds try to be more respectful of their friends' feelings. They will usually ask to try out an activity or to use something instead of grabbing it away from a friend.

For play to continue and friendships to be maintained, actions need to be satisfying for all of the children. For instance, when Becky, Elise, and Rosa play beauty spa, Becky always wants to be the "massager" and the beautician. She tells the other girls, "You are my clients." A problem can arise when one friend, like Becky, always needs to dominate the play activity. In this case, Elise and Rosa become frustrated because they do not want to follow Becky's orders all of the time. Feeling stressed, Rosa threatens Becky: "You can't come to my birthday party if I can't polish nails." Rosa leaves with hurt feelings.

While establishing their social identities, four-year-olds begin to show a preference for same-sex friendships. This does not mean, however, that if Anna and Nick ride to school together in a carpool, they cannot be best friends. In fact, they might even develop a little crush on each other.

This is an exciting time in the preschoolers' social development. They enter into intense, intimate relationships with a best friend. Some of these preschool attachments last for many years. My best nursery school pal, Elizabeth Marcy, and I remained friends well into adulthood, and I was the maid of honor at her wedding!

Best friends may appear inseparable. They like to sit next to each other and whisper secrets back and forth. They giggle while they walk with their arms around each other. Best friends enjoy laughing at each other's silly jokes. In mutual admiration, two soccer buddies, Paula and Tracy, each wear their hair in duplicate ponytails tied back with purple ribbons. Best friends Deepak and Arnold like to dress alike in their matching Spurs shirts and wristbands. Rituals are also part of these ongoing best-friend relationships. Upon arrival at school, Alec and Kenny high-five each other twice. Then, they laugh as they greet each other with "Hello, Jell-O!" and head off together for the block corner, their favorite play area.

At this age, best-friend relationships easily cross racial and cultural lines. Special friendships also may be formed with adults. Jon became very attached to our center's foster grandmother, Mrs. Metzger. Daily, the two of them made pretend sundaes for their "ice cream social." This important intergenerational friendship helped Jon learn how to relate to others.

It takes two committed friends to support a best-friend relationship. When problems arise, they may need to use their problem-solving skills or try compromising. Mary Ann explains to Debbie carefully, "For our Cinderella party, if you give me the diamond tiara to wear this time, I'll give you the beautiful fur cape."

As marvelous as it is to have a best friend, it can be devastating if a seemingly insurmountable problem arises. When Erica arrives at circle time, she finds Angie sitting in her special place next to Kimberly. And they are laughing and hugging each other! It is difficult for Erica to perceive that her very best friend, Kimberly, could like someone else as much as her. Jealous and feeling excluded by the presence of this third child, she yells back to Kimberly, "You are not my best friend anymore!" Usually, best friends manage to make up. However, mending hurt feelings can be hard, and the children may decide to just move on. Even though these situations may be unpleasant, it is part of the larger process of making friends and learning different ways to manage relationships.

What You Can Do

■ **Show how to approach a friend.** Often, young children do not know how to initiate a friendship. Model suggestions and give them verbal hints. Show them how to give a friendly smile or inviting wave. They can say hello and use the friend's name: "Hello, Roberto!" They might add, "Come play with me." Help them consider bringing along an item to add interest when trying to join in the play.

■ **Model positive friendship behaviors.** Work out unpleasant interpersonal situations using puppets. Show how a friendly puppet might respond to an unlikeable puppet who teases or tries to take away a toy. The friendly puppet could explain, "I'm playing with the robot now. But you can have it next."

■ **Engineer the environment.** Bring friends together by designing collaborative interest centers. Encourage pair play by adding two phones or two fascinating hats in the dramatic play center. Side-by-side chairs at the computer center will stimulate game playing.

■ **Create friendship posters.** Take pictures of friends interacting together. Then blow them up to decorate your classroom walls. Ask the children to provide friendship captions by dictating a phrase for you to write down about what they are doing together.

■ **Nominate a friend.** During circle time, invite children to state a characteristic of a good friend (such as kind or fun). Write the suggestions on chart paper. Then encourage children to put a friend's name on a strip of paper next to the trait. This can be an ongoing activity.

Other Aspects to Consider—Alerts

■ **Help children cope with feelings of loss.** Young children often feel sad when a friend moves away, switches schools, or is assigned to another class. If a child becomes severely depressed, you and the parents may need to find ways for the friends to stay in touch and maintain their friendship (such as sending photo postcards or meeting for a picnic). If the depression continues to lead to an unhealthy emotional state, the parents might need to seek assistance from a therapist.

- **Watch for excessive competition or bullying.** Difficulties with the relationship can occur when one friend takes a leadership role and expects that his buddy will always want to follow along with his ideas. This may cause a falling out between the two friends. It is important to be aware of any bullying tactics being used by the more dominant friend.
- **Monitor overlooked or excluded children's feelings.** Sometimes children can be unkind by socially rejecting a specific child. Her feelings can be hurt when she is ignored or always selected last to play. She may need assistance socially with attempts at making friends and joining play activities.

ACTIVITIES FOR PARENTS TO TRY AT HOME

- **Arrange for play dates.** Invite friends to play with your child at home or at the park. Give your child an opportunity to test out and develop his social skills in a comfortable environment with you nearby for support.
- **Offer cooperative and turn-taking activities.** Help your child learn to make friends and play with others by offering games and activities, such as Candyland or two-person catch. Share cooking experiences, such as pouring and beating the milk while creating pudding together for a yummy snack and good conversation.

- ■ **Decorate friendship valentines.** Provide art materials so your child can show her friends how much she likes them. Why not create and send valentines to special friends all year long? The notes might say, "You are my friend because. . . ." Encourage her to sign her name and then deliver the friendly messages.
- ■ **Cultivate intergenerational friends.** It's important for your child to have friends of all ages. He might learn a skill, such as how to hammer nails, from your neighbor, then help that neighbor by shoveling snow. On a weekly trip visiting an assisted living center, your daughter might learn about plants as she gardens with a senior friend. And your son can develop a long-distance friendship when he gathers materials for care packages to ship to military personnel overseas.
- ■ **Bring home a four-legged friend.** Consider adopting a rescue dog. This special-situation puppy needs love and care and will eagerly befriend your child. My two grandsons, Owen and Adam, have loved their experiences adopting furry friends. Onyx and Bruno have helped both boys discover the joy of their dogs' loyalty and have helped to teach them how to handle responsibility.

RELATED BOOKS TO READ WITH CHILDREN

Alborough, Jez. 2001. *My Friend Bear.* Cambridge, MA: Candlewick Press.

Hutchins, Pat. 1993. *My Best Friend.* New York: Greenwillow Books.

Lobel, Arnold. 1979. *Frog and Toad Are Friends.* New York: HarperCollins.

Marshall, James. 2008. *George and Martha: The Complete Stories of Two Best Friends, Collector's Edition.* Boston: HMH Books for Young Readers.

Munson, Derek. 2000. *Enemy Pie.* San Francisco: Chronicle Books.

2

LEARNING TO
SHARE AND COOPERATE

Sharing—an action that enables someone to take a turn using or enjoying something that belongs to another person

Cooperation—a process that involves people working together and being helpful to accomplish something

An inability to share can spark conflicts among young preschoolers, and a willingness to share can promote positive relationships and fun play experiences. Naturally, not all children develop these skills at the same age or to the same degree, but these snapshots will help you know what you can probably expect to see as sharing and cooperation evolve:

- Three-year-olds have difficulty sharing personal possessions.
- Three-year-olds feel that they don't have to share if they have the object first.
- Three-year-olds sometimes may not want to share their teacher's attention.
- Four-year-olds easily share ideas and materials during cooperative play.
- Four-year-olds experiment with taking turns and trading objects.
- Four-year-olds are beginning to learn how to negotiate.

Now let's take a look at some of the types of challenges that might arise in the classroom as preschoolers are faced with sharing issues and opportunities to play cooperatively.

All curled up on her rest mat, Emma, a young three-year-old, snuggles with her teddy that she brought from home. Settling in comfortably, she rubs the ears of Bear-Bear. When Mia reaches over to pat Emma's cherished bear, too, Emma cries out, "No! Bear-Bear is mine!" Then she hugs him tightly to keep Mia from touching him. Because her nana gave her the bear, it is very special to Emma, and she has no intention of sharing her prized personal possession.

Emma's teacher, Mrs. Lopez, intercedes and tells Mia, "Emma needs to hold her special Bear-Bear. It is important to help her rest. We'll find you another soft teddy bear to cuddle so you can nap, too."

When three-year-olds, like Emma, identify strongly with a possession, they feel almost as if they are giving away a portion of themselves if they have to share the item. Mrs. Lopez treats Emma's anxiety with respect because she understands Emma is not yet socially or emotionally ready to share something this personal. Emma needs to feel secure about her ownership of the bear. She must feel comfortable that if another child touches or borrows her toy, it will come back to her. Still very egocentric, Emma does not yet feel that it is okay for others to play with Bear-Bear, even temporarily.

The concept of sharing becomes even more difficult for Emma to understand during play time, when Mrs. Lopez tells Emma she must give the xylophone to Galina and let her have a turn. Emma exclaims, "I had it first! It's mine now!" Because Emma physically possesses the instrument, she truly believes that she alone has the right to play with it. Mrs. Lopez patiently tries to explain to the girls, "Toys and things that belong to the school must be shared by all of the children at the school."

Sharing can indeed be confusing for young three-year-olds, who find it difficult to see a situation from another's point of view. For instance, Gunner waits unwillingly while his teacher holds a cup very still for Marvin as he slowly pours juice from a pitcher. Gunner wants her to help him too, and he doesn't want to share her attention. Gunner becomes even more impatient when his teacher tells him he has to wait his turn.

While three-year-olds Elsa and Callie play together outside, Elsa hands Callie a pretty stone that she found. Callie smiles and taps it with her finger. Then Elsa gives her another stone. Callie bangs the two stones together. Both girls laugh at the clacking sound.

Because the rocks do not actually belong to Elsa, she does not feel threatened as she initiates sharing these items with Callie. Unlike Emma and her prized Bear-Bear, Elsa does not have a vested interest in the rocks, so she feels empowered to test out the sharing process. During this simple interactive activity, the girls discover that sharing and playing cooperatively can be fun.

When preschoolers reach three and a half years old, through time and practice they begin to feel a little more comfortable making decisions about sharing. Now that they have learned that lending an item is a temporary situation, they are not quite so protective of the materials they are sharing. They may even spontaneously begin to share if they know something will be returned. On the other hand, they will be quite stressed if someone takes something they are playing with without asking permission. And they certainly will not be pleased if another child tries to keep the borrowed object permanently.

Tossing a bean bag back and forth, young preschoolers Nicky and Ling are enjoying their simple cooperative game. It is fairly easy for the boys to relate to each other one-on-one as they share the bean bag. When a third child attempts to join in, however, it becomes rather overwhelming for them to take turns and share the bean bag. They may even exclude the newcomer from the activity.

In contrast, four-year-olds tend to be eager to share without even being asked, especially if they are enthusiastic about working on a small project together with their buddies. For instance, as these preschoolers are intensely involved in an assembly line fashion in their "fast food restaurant," they chant, "Burgers on the buns; pickles on the burgers." Their self-initiated cooperative effort involves fascinating dialogue paired with lots of action. Zoe shares her idea for how to create a luscious, round hamburger bun by pressing down on playdough with a biscuit cutter. Lily and Emily take turns exchanging kitchen equipment, such as tongs and a slotted spoon, to cook their french fries perfectly. These make-believe chefs learn that it's exciting to share ideas, real materials, and each other's company in a cooperative venture.

By the time they become four, preschoolers discover that they are sharing almost everything with their friends. They love sharing silly riddles and outlandish jokes. They adore sharing outrageous stories with each other about mile-high skyscrapers or a kingdom of miniature dinosaurs. Job sharing is fun too, as they cooperatively create a human chain to rapidly stack a heap of blocks back on the shelves.

While working on projects, problems often arise when several children wish to use the same materials. As Caden and Logan play auto repair shop, they each want the single wrench. In an attempt to solve their problem, Logan offers an enticing trade to Caden. "How about I give you two radiator hoses if I can have the wrench?" Older four-year-olds are beginning to learn how to negotiate. Sometimes they go to great lengths to get something. Caden needs Logan's new tire for his car. He offers to show Logan how to change his battery while adding a little bribe to up the ante. "You can go to the Six Flags Water Park with me this weekend if I can have your tire." Logan agrees.

Because four-year-olds are empathetic, they are able to share their feelings with each other. Suzanne tells her best friend Claire, "I am feeling sad because my daddy's being sent overseas with the Army." Claire hugs her friend and says, "I understand. My papa and mema took their RV back home to Florida. I miss them a lot." The girls feel a little better after they share some markers for drawing and create cards to let their special relatives know how much they love and miss them.

What You Can Do

- **Arrange for activities to share.** Place a huge ball of homemade playdough in the center of a table. Encourage children to break off pieces and make something exciting together. Put materials on shelves at eye level with easy access so preschoolers can quickly spot items to play with and share together, such as board games, farm-animal figurines, or Bristle Blocks.

- **Offer cooperative activities.** Suggest some activities that don't require tangible materials. Children could try singing hand-clapping chants and add-on songs, such as "There Was an Old Lady Who Swallowed a Fly." Try noncompetitive activities, such as having a bucket brigade to fill the sandbox or turning the egg beater to whip up pretend cream or create butter. Help preschoolers focus on having fun while sharing activities and working together.

Social Development of Three- and Four-Year-Olds

- **Make games of sharing.** When there is only one piece of equipment available, encourage young children to brainstorm what to do. With one wagon, children might take turns riding and pulling. Or they could fill the wagon with toys. Then some might push while others pull. Children could create a share-a-song; one friend starts the song, then the other finishes it. Model how to use silly words or rhyming sounds, such as "Row, row, row your boat/Putting on your coat."
- **Work out a sharing system.** Young preschoolers worry about a friend keeping something forever. Try setting a timer. Explain that the loaned item comes back after she hears the buzzer. Knowing when a turn will be over may encourage a child to share another time.
- **Temporarily remove a problem object.** During my first year as a preschool teacher, one yellow and three red tricycles were delivered. No matter what we tried, everyone always wanted the yellow trike, and squabbles ensued. After retiring the yellow trike several times, we finally painted it red! Years later, we still refer to an impasse situation as a "yellow-trike event"!

OTHER ASPECTS TO CONSIDER—ALERTS

- **Do not demand that a child share.** Sharing is not always a realistic expectation for young children. Actually, you might inspire anger or resentment if you pressure him by saying such things as "Don't be selfish." "You are acting greedy." "Nice boys share!" Give him a choice about sharing. Respect where children are developmentally.
- **Learning styles and individual temperaments influence a child's ability to cooperate and share.** When a child has strong interpersonal skills or is reflective, she may quite naturally demonstrate generosity. Others who do not possess these traits may exhibit a more difficult time cooperating and sharing.
- **A young child may not wish to share a personal item.** If a child cannot bear to lend certain personal objects from home, such as his favorite blanket that he uses to go to sleep or a special doll that is a present from his aunt, you need to help the other child find a suitable substitute item to play with so she feels she has your support. The child may need to place his personal possession away in a designated safe place when not using it so as not to tempt other children.

ACTIVITIES FOR PARENTS TO TRY AT HOME

- **Help initiate sharing.** Do not overwhelm your young child. Start out very basically to make it easy to share with a friend. Offer a simple form puzzle or four-piece puzzle for the friends to put together. Then stimulate sharing by increasing the complexity of the materials offered; you might add miniature cars to go with Lego bricks or plastic cups to play with in the sandbox.

- **Develop basic rules.** Discuss things your child may not want to share, such as his favorite truck he got for his birthday. Think about things he is willing to share, such as fingerpaints or wooden blocks. Talk about how important it is for everybody to ask permission before taking others' belongings or things they are working with. To reinforce the rules, complement him when he remembers to ask first.

- **Use duplicates to increase cooperation.** Because it is quite difficult for young preschoolers to share and play cooperatively with others, arrange to have extras of interesting toys, such as sand pails or fire helmets, during play dates. Using duplicate old cell phones as props could inspire great cooperative conversations. It's much more pleasant for children to not always have to wait for a turn.

- **Enjoy cooperative jobs.** Have fun working together to perform household tasks. See how fast they go! For instance, have your child sweep while you hold the dust pan. One person can spray water on a dirty window as the other wipes it clean with a paper towel. Be spontaneous.

- **Participate in community sharing.** Provide your child with art supplies so she can create cheerful holiday decorations for seniors' trays for Meals on Wheels deliveries. Help her sort out toys, books, and clothes to donate to needy families at the homeless shelter or to another relief organization. Wash old towels to share with the American Society for the Prevention of Cruelty to Animals for soft animal bedding.

RELATED BOOKS TO READ WITH CHILDREN

Dewdney, Anna. 2012. *Llama Llama Time to Share*. New York: Viking.

Hoberman, Mary Ann. 2000. *One of Each*. Boston: Little, Brown Books for Young Readers.

Hutchins, Pat. 1989. *The Doorbell Rang*. New York: Greenwillow Books.

Lionni, Leo. 1996. *It's Mine!* New York: Dragonfly Books.

Rosen, Michael. 2005. *This Is Our House*. Cambridge, MA: Candlewick Press.

3

CREATING
HAPPINESS

Happiness—a pleasurable, satisfying experience and feeling that life is good

Expressing emotions comes naturally to preschoolers, although their ability to do so verbally develops at different rates. Whether they are accomplishing a new task, spending time with people they love, or laughing with friends, you will know it when they are feeling good. Some of the following types of reactions are relatively common among three- and four-year-olds:

- Three-year-olds are elated when their teacher or parents spend special time with just them.
- Three-year-olds are happy when they are treated like big boys and girls.
- Three-and-a-half-year-olds are sometimes unhappy and may appear worried and stressed.
- Four-year-olds love focusing passionately on things they are intensely interested in.
- Four-year-olds are happy when they expand their social relationships by interacting with their friends.
- Four-year-olds feel positive when they accomplish something and make a contribution.

Now let's look at some of the types of interactions you might see in your classroom as children express unhappiness or joy in response to what is going on around them.

Adam, who is just turning four, is so happy that his smile reaches from ear to ear. He enthusiastically hops up and down until he gets Ms. Fanger's attention, then he blurts out, "Guess what? Guess what?" She smiles back at him and asks, "What?" Without stopping, Adam eagerly announces, "It's my birthday. Daddy is getting me today. We're going to buy my Aquaman cake. Then—just us—are picking out a rescued puppy. I can't wait to hug my

own birthday puppy. And feed her. And teach her tricks!"

Adam's euphoric appearance with his big smile and jubilant bouncing indicates his extreme happiness with his life at the moment. Because three-year-olds and young four-year-olds are still egocentric, they are interested in most things having to do with themselves. Obviously, Adam's birthday is very important to him, along with "my" Aquaman cake and "my" puppy. A child of this age is elated when a parent or teacher spends special time with just him. He is also delighted with surprises and treats, such as a new puppy to hug and care for. Being given a special responsibility, such as feeding a dog, makes a preschooler feel happy to be treated like a big boy.

In Ms. Lopez's classroom, three-and-a-half-year-old Carla is frowning and working on a difficult puzzle. Unsure, Carla keeps turning pieces various ways. When Ms. Lopez sits down next to her, she encourages Carla's manipulations. After Carla completes the challenging puzzle, she claps her hands joyfully. Ms. Lopez smiles and gives Carla a warm, congratulatory hug.

Some preschoolers around the age of three and a half appear to worry about things and may seem stressed. They may stutter a little, appear uncoordinated, and seem unsure of themselves. Socially and emotionally, they sometimes seem rather unhappy and might require additional attention from their teachers and parents to assist them in reducing their anxiety.

Preschoolers are learning that with practice and persistence they may eventually be able to solve a problem or gain control of a situation. This experience enables them to work toward feeling successful and happy with their own efforts. When Carla receives inspiration and positive feedback from her teacher, she is thrilled. Three-year-olds especially are delighted when special adults in their lives sit close and concentrate on them by playing games or sharing books with them. These particular moments help young children feel connected to some of their favorite people, and those connections in turn produce feelings of security, trust, and self-confidence. These are all experiences that build a preschooler's sense of happiness.

In another social situation, four-year-old Nathan is thrilled about showing his new castle model to his best friend, Chung. Chung has declared Nathan "the castle king" because Nathan knows so much about medieval times. With great excitement, they operate the drawbridge and raise the flags over the turrets. Then they enthusiastically ask each other questions and discuss how to go about setting up a jousting tournament. Next, they use their ideas to create knights and horses using Lego bricks. Finally, they construct a funny ferocious dragon for the castle garden. They enjoy sharing a laughing jag as they call out silly names for their medieval flamethrower!

Although three-year-olds find great joy in connecting with the special adults in their lives, four-year-olds are ever so happy expanding their social relationships by interacting with friends—especially best friends. If they gain recognition from their peers, such as when Chung identified Nathan as the castle king, they feel valued. This, of course, can raise the child's self-esteem. When given the opportunity to collect information and ask lots of questions with their buddies, the ever-so-curious four-year-olds are at their happiest. Four-year-olds love focusing passionately on things they are intensely interested in, such as Nathan's and Chung's fascination with castles and dragons. However, they could also be just as happily engaged playing with other children while enhancing their physical skills when digging and hoeing to create a vegetable garden.

Frequently, gung-ho four-year-olds are positively giddy as they become carried away with their enthusiasm, just like the boys with their funny flame-throwing dragon. All fired up by their silliness, they almost seem to spin out of control with their loud laughter and shrieks of joy. When a preschooler smiles, his brain receives a message from his facial muscles. And laughter releases a chemical into his body that contributes to the child's feeling of happiness.

Two girls in another classroom are helping to clean up the art area. Lashonda and Ella are washing the sticky tables with sponges and soapy water. When Lashonda can't find the paper towels to dry the tables, she becomes sad and upset. "Don't worry," says Ella. "I know where they are." Smiling, they proudly finish their assigned job together.

Preschoolers enjoy taking on meaningful jobs at school and home. They are very happy when they please their friends, teachers, and parents by doing such things as helping with cleaning the table or picking up toys. It makes them feel positive and independent when they achieve something and make a contribution.

During circle time, Ms. Chomicky asks her preschoolers to think really hard about what makes them happiest. Immediately, hands shoot up. Kyle responds, "Having lots of fun playing!" His classmates nod in agreement. Mateo tells about climbing high on the playground equipment with Joshua. Ressa describes how she and Skyler make playdough pizza pies, then pretend to eat them.

High on most preschoolers' lists are experiences with hands-on activities and making connections with their friends. They are happiest when they have lots of time for involvement in unstructured play. They particularly love engaging in active play outdoors. All of these activities encourage them to happily use their imaginations.

Being involved with these healthy experiences enables young children to discover the importance of long-term happiness, instead of the short-term rush they experience with costly video games or toys, such as a talking robot, that they soon tire of. Four-year-olds particularly are delighted by playing for hours on end with their favorite collections, such as miniature cars, farm animal figurines, or colorful sea shells from the beach, instead of a lot of expensive toys that are not developmentally appropriate. A special inner glow of gratitude appears when young children have teachers or parents spend time helping them use their imaginations to make wonderful creations, such as building a super race car using scrap wood at the workbench.

What You Can Do

- **Help children make a difference.** Children feel happy when they are doing things for others. Provide opportunities for them to handle responsibility and be recognized for their efforts. For example, encourage them to participate in spring cleanup. Outside, they could wash the trikes or rake up leaves into a huge pile; inside, they could race to find missing puzzle pieces in the manipulative bins or scrub down the paint easels. Have a celebration when the school is all spruced up. Encourage them to bring joy to others. Offer supplies so they can decorate fancy bookmarks to donate to a children's hospital or senior living center.

- **Promote mastering a skill.** Encourage children to practice a skill. Help them persist until they feel successful. For example, when a child learns to balance on and ride a scooter, she feels competent and thrilled with her accomplishments.

- **Use a sense of humor.** Model how you handle your frustration and don't give up on a task. Help children think of solutions if they get stuck. Be able to laugh at yourself if you mess up. If you smile, the children will learn to smile as well. Smiling is contagious! For instance, if it rains for your picnic, construct picnic benches in the block area and spread a big tablecloth inside on the floor. Bon appétit!

- **Design a happiness center.** Offer markers, glue sticks, scissors, and magazines, so that children can cut smiling faces out of magazines and glue a huge group together into a smiling-face collage. Together, create a giant book of riddles and jokes. Ask parents and other school visitors to contribute their favorite humorous ideas. Or let children make happy-face headbands by drawing or attaching smiley faces on folded cloth or stretchy bands.

- **Create a happiness wall.** Ask children to draw pictures of things that make them happy, such as playing ball with their friends or fishing with their fathers. Use the class camera to snap photos of happy days, and then display them for discussion. Develop a graph showing how many classmates find happiness in activities such as singing, eating popcorn, or tickling a buddy.

OTHER ASPECTS TO CONSIDER—ALERTS

- **Check the child's health if he seems constantly unhappy.** If a child does not get enough sleep on a regular basis, he can become irritable. A child will feel healthier and happier if he gets at least an hour of exercise daily. If a child comes to school hungry or he never has enough to eat, his body may actually hurt. It is also difficult for him to feel good if his diet consists of lots of inappropriate foods (such as candy or soda). Certain allergies set off alarms inside individual children's bodies, which can make them feel miserable and unhappy.

- **Investigate if a child is always unhappy during play time or seems to be feeling left out.** Observe her interactions with others. Is she too timid to join play activities? Or is she bossy and a bully that no one wants to play with? Is she happiest playing by herself? Be aware of her temperament. Help to model ways to work with others. Smile and laugh when you interact with children. Provide opportunities for a shy child to start off interacting gradually, perhaps by pairing her with an older child or by rolling a ball back and forth.

- **Do not overpraise.** A child is happy when he masters and experiences activities, such as running, hopping, and wiggling through a maze with friends. However, if you always say "good job" whether he completes a task well or not, he will become confused. He will be happier if you let him know you appreciate his efforts along the way as he tries to master something, rather than always praising the finished product.

ACTIVITIES FOR PARENTS TO TRY AT HOME

- **Listen to your child.** Your child is ever so happy when you really listen to him and tune into what he is saying and doing. He adores having you spend one-on-one time with him. He feels very happy when you play his special games (such as Old Maid) and spend time with him in his favorite spots (for example, a fort made with your bedroom comforter). You'll get big smiles for these precious moments!

- **Provide simple, happy experiences.** Have fun at the public library picking out books to read together. Then, laugh out loud at some silly stories, such as *Green Eggs and Ham* by Dr. Seuss. Afterward, scramble some green eggs for a family breakfast. Help your child  understand that she doesn't need expensive toys and materials to be happy and have fun.

- **Ensure consistency.** Provide a calm, regular bedtime for your child. Make sure you have a relaxing routine for family meals. If your child is well rested and his tummy is full, he is on his way to feeling satisfied and happy.

- **Create happy and sad puppets.** On one side of a paper plate, encourage your child to draw a happy face. Make a sad face on the other side. If your child is having a hard time expressing her feelings, she can manipulate the plate to whichever side shows how she feels. Play a happy-sad game. Tell little stories. Then ask your puppeteer to hold up the side that shows how the character is feeling. Can she tell you why the character is happy or sad?

- **Have wet and wild outdoor fun!** Put on bathing suits during hot weather and step outside. Soak squishy foam balls in water. Enjoy a lively game of catch. What a great happy feeling as your child cools off with splashes of water.

Social Development of Three- and Four-Year-Olds

Related Books to Read with Children

Dyer, Wayne W., with Kristina Tracy. 2005. *Incredible You! 10 Ways to Let Your Greatness Shine Through.* Carlsbad, CA: Hay House.

Foreman, Jack, and Michael Foreman. 2008. *Say Hello.* Cambridge, MA: Candlewick Press.

Menchin, Scott. 2007. *Taking a Bath with the Dog and Other Things That Make Me Happy.* Cambridge, MA: Candlewick Press.

Rath, Tom, and Mary Reckmeyer. 2009. *How Full Is Your Bucket? For Kids.* New York: Gallup Press.

Rosenthal, Amy Krouse, and Tom Lichtenheld. 2009. *Yes Day!* New York: HarperCollins Children's Books.

Tullet, Hervé. 2011. *Press Here.* San Francisco: Chronicle Books.

DEALING WITH
TEASING

Teasing—making fun of someone in a playful manner or attempting to provoke someone in an unkind or annoying way

As preschoolers start to explore teasing behaviors, you will see a range of positive and negative expressions of teasing. Although not all children develop at the same rate, you are likely to see some of the following types of teasing behaviors among three- and four-year-olds:

- Three-year-olds enjoy teasing tickle play and "gotcha" games.
- Three-year-olds sometimes have difficulty understanding how the other person might be feeling during teasing.
- Three-year-olds are frequently sensitive and vulnerable to teasing and having their feelings hurt.
- Four-year-olds often use name-calling as a way to socially reject and exclude others.
- Four-year-olds feel empowered using inappropriate language for its shock value when they tease others.

- Four-year-olds frequently get carried away with teasing because they have difficulty distinguishing between real-life and make-believe situations and actions.

These types of behaviors show up in the classroom in different ways. The following anecdotes explore positive and negative teasing interactions that might occur in a pre-schooler's world.

Happy sounds are radiating from the three-year-old room as Ms. Packer laughs and teases Stella. In a cheery, singsong voice, Ms. Packer chants, "I've got your nose!" Then, she shows Stella her thumb sticking out from the next two fingers made into a fist. Stella giggles as she tries to capture her pretend nose and put it back on her face.

This type of teasing is a form of play that can be lots of fun when both parties involved are enjoying themselves. However, as soon as one of the players becomes stressed or hurt and they are no longer having a good time, the teasing ceases to be fun. For instance, if Stella tries to replicate this fun activity with her friend, Alice, and pinches her nose hard enough to make her yell out, the teasing becomes unpleasant. When three-year-olds initiate teasing on their own, it is frequently unsuccessful because they simply are not sophisticated enough to know what makes it funny or effective. It is difficult for them to understand how the other person might be feeling.

Young children, like Stella, learn how to behave socially and discover ways to interact with others by imitating their parents, teachers, and peers. For example, when Valeria's mom says, "You are my baby," it is meant as a gentle tease and a tender term of endearment. On the other hand, it is quite different if four-year-old Oliver mimics his older brother and calls his classmate Logan a baby because he likes to sit next to the teacher. Then, when Oliver follows this up with a verbal tease, "Baby, baby, stick your head in gravy," it becomes a mean taunt.

Logan gets his feelings hurt and becomes angry. He then retorts to Oliver, "You are a poop head!"

When Jamar doesn't want to allow Lei, a three-and-a-half-year-old, to join in the soccer game with the four-year-old boys, he teases him by calling out, "Flip-flop, flip-flop. Trip-trop, trip-trop! You need sneakers. You can't play with stupid flip-flops!" Feeling embarrassed and sad, Lei turns around and walks off the field, crying.

Four-year-olds, like Jamar, can be quite bossy and like to show off their power and gain attention by belittling others. They frequently use name-calling as a way to socially reject others. This particular type of teasing is often used to exclude others and can be a form of bullying. It is meant to ensure that a particular child is left out of an activity. Children exclude others for many reasons, such as their appearance, their age, or where they live. Sadly, most of the time a child has no control over these reasons.

During a stage of disequilibrium in young children's development, they may appear out of sorts. You might notice that they frustrate easily or seem very sensitive. During this stage, which occurs at about age three and a half, children can feel particularly vulnerable to being teased. When a child this age, like Lei, has his feelings hurt, he is apt to become upset because he does not understand teasing and why someone would want to be so mean to him. His egocentrism forces him to focus on himself.

By age four, preschoolers start to understand and take advantage of the effects that teasing can have on their peers, just like when the TV character Bart Simpson relishes telling his sister Lisa, "Eat my shorts." They enjoy using inappropriate language for its shock value. For example, Timmy greets his buddy Daniel at the door by asking him, "Can you say 'hi' to your knee?" Daniel responds, "Sure. Hi, knee." Timmy starts to howl with laughter. He shakes his finger at Daniel and says, "You said a bad word. You said *heinie!*" In this case, because four-year-olds think that using potty language and shocking others is funny, they enjoy this verbal tease together.

At other times, four-year-olds like to feel empowered or gain attention by annoying others through targeting them with inappropriate language, such as toilet talk and swear words. Not too far removed from toilet training, they are still intrigued with their bodily functions. For instance, Jacob is jealous because he thinks Dylan always gets to hold the door. Therefore, Jacob tries to antagonize Dylan by singing, "If you're happy and you know it poop on Dylan's head!" Upset and feeling uncomfortable with the teasing and because she interprets Jacob's words literally, three-year-old Caroline pouts and says, "No! That is not right. Sing 'Clap your hands.'"

Liking to be in control while also displaying their whimsical sense of humor, four-year-olds sometimes react to an adult's request with a teasing verbal response that might not be acceptable to adults. For example, when asked by her teacher to put away the rhythm instruments on the music carts, Zoey grins. Attempting to assert her independence, she responds by mimicking teasing phrases that she's heard her older brother use. "No way, José. Much later alligator!" Surprised, Zoey's teacher gives her a puzzled look.

We know that it is difficult for energetic preschoolers to sit still next to one another for very long if they must wait during transition times. With their short attention spans, it is not uncommon for them to begin to tease each other in nonverbal ways by bumping shoulders or pretending to poke each other and then pulling away. This teasing play can be fun, just as long as it doesn't escalate and spiral out of control. Other nonverbal teasing games during which children enjoy interacting socially are tickling activities, making silly faces, and playing tag as the participants dodge one another and switch roles.

Because so many preschoolers spend hours in front of TV and computer screens, this is how they see and learn about people reacting toward others. Unfortunately, many of the interactions are not respectful or caring. They observe characters interacting with mean-spirited teasing and antisocial behaviors that get out of hand. For example, Luis runs away with Emilio's favorite Boston Red Sox baseball cap. Teasing him, Luis yells, "Slow poke, you're a joke. You can't catch me!" Annoyed, Emilio responds, "But the Ninja Turtles can get you!" At first, Emilio pretends to karate chop Luis's head and back. Then, really upset because Luis doesn't release the hat, Emilio actually karate chops Luis's hand and kicks him before grabbing his hat back.

Using TV and movie characters as models of social behavior is problematic for young children. Often, it is difficult for them to understand the line between fantasy and real-life situations. The more time they spend with inappropriate screen images, the less time they have to actually spend learning how to work things out by building social relationships positively through their own creative play as problem solvers.

What You Can Do

- **Let the teased child know you care.** Assure her that you are there with your support to help her work through the problem if someone is hurting her feelings or is excluding her from a situation. Reassure her that this is not tattling. Pair the victimized child up with a buddy or give her a special job, such as holding the flag, so she feels like part of the group.
- **Talk about it.** Create two playdough figures so you can address the problem together and play out a situation that has upset the teased child. Listen carefully to the child's perspective.
- **Empower the teased child to stand up for himself.** If a child teases him by saying, "Hey, stinky boy!" encourage the teased child to say firmly, "My name is Craig."
- **Redirect inappropriate teasing.** If you see that children are playfully teasing by smacking each other on the back, but then it begins to escalate, consider getting out the punching bag. When a preschooler teases and substitutes curse words in a favorite song, suggest trying the song with silly rhyming words instead.
- **Validate a child's feelings.** Even though you may not approve of how a preschooler handles a problem, you can explain to her that you understand how she feels. For example, if one

child pesters another by following her everywhere and then wants to share her computer, it can be annoying. However, instead of allowing the annoyed child to taunt the follower with teasing insults to go away, model for the indignant child more appropriate ways to handle the situation. The child could simply say, "Inez, stop following me. I want to sit by myself."

- **Be clear that bullies are not allowed!** Read *King of the Playground* by Phyllis Naylor as a springboard for a discussion about how the group feels about bullies. Talk about some reasons children might tease—maybe because someone is different? Draw some posters that say "No bullies!" and hang them around the classroom as reminders.

OTHER ASPECTS TO CONSIDER—ALERTS

- **Be aware of excessive use of inappropriate language.** As preschoolers experiment with language and its effects on people, it is normal for them to occasionally use potty words, descriptive body words, or swear words. However, if they continually use inappropriate language as a means of teasing others to hurt their feelings or embarrass them, have a discussion about how this behavior is unacceptable. It might be helpful to talk about or dramatize how this type of teasing makes others feel.

- **Is a child giving you messages he's being harassed?** Does a child complain he doesn't want to come to school or that he has a tummy ache each morning? Does he avoid playing with a certain child or complain that he is being teased by her? Observe to see if teasing is getting out of hand, prolonged, or stressful for this child. Be sure not to downplay the effect with messages such as "It'll be okay. She's only teasing." Let the concerned child know that you will intervene and help him work out the problem. Help the harassing child understand that bullying is never acceptable behavior.

- **Watch out for scripted play that makes others unhappy.** When you see preschoolers spending much of their time using irritating, teasing scripted language, actions, or toy characters from TV programs, movies, or computer games, redirect them to other activities where they can develop their own dialogues and social interactions. Provide interesting props to stimulate cooperative play in the construction center or dramatic play area.

Activities for Parents to Try at Home

- **Practice not being a victim.** Act out what your child should do if being teased. Help children practice acting out these suggestions: Ignore the tease and walk away. Don't be alone; stay near others. Don't overreact. Pretend the teaser is invisible.

- **Figure out why your child is teasing others.** Have there been any life changes for her, such as a new baby, a divorce, or a grandparent moving in? Is she teasing others because she is jealous or wants attention? Is she targeting a specific child because she looks different or acts different? Let the teacher know so you can all work together to change this behavior.

- **Provide a positive atmosphere at home.** Be observant and make sure that your child is not being teased unnecessarily by older siblings. Often this can carry over to school, where your child will mimic siblings' behavior. Make sure when you are playing teasing games with your child, such as tummy tickling, that you don't take it too far, especially if your child is very sensitive.

- **Be aware of your language.** As you know, your child will imitate what you say. So if you use inappropriate words to tease a friend on the phone or your spouse while he's driving, it could be repeated at school. Or think about your language, meant as a tease, while you watch a football game on TV. Model positive language in front of your child.

- **Have fun with silly words.** When nonstop bathroom language, such as "You are a pee-pee-poopy spider," drives you up the wall, try creating funny rhymes instead: "You are a silly Adam Badam." You can sit together and read silly words in books. You'll find yourselves laughing about Pam Adams's book *There Was an Old Lady Who Swallowed a Fly* when reading that it "wriggled and wriggled and jiggled inside her."

Books to Share with Children

Adams, Pam. 2003. *There Was an Old Lady Who Swallowed a Fly*. Swindon, UK: Child's Play International.

Bracken, Beth. 2012. *The Little Bully*. North Mankato, MN: Picture Window Books.

Dewdney, Anna. 2013. *Llama, Llama and the Bully Goat*. New York: Viking Books for Young Readers.

Emberley, Ed. 2007. *Bye-Bye, Big Bad Bullybug!* New York: L B Kids.

Lovell, Patty. 2001. *Stand Tall, Molly Lou Melon*. New York: G. P. Putnam's Sons.

Naylor, Phyllis Reynolds. 1991. *King of the Playground*. New York: Atheneum.

O'Neill, Alexis. 2002. *The Recess Queen*. New York: Scholastic.

5

PARTICIPATING IN ROUGH-AND-TUMBLE PLAY

Rough-and-tumble play—lively and playful physical interactions of a social nature that develop positive, exuberant feelings among the participants

Although rough-and-tumble play, or roughhousing, often gets a bad rap from teachers and parents, it can be beneficial in the development of many preschool skills. At its best, it is fun and brings pleasure to the participants. To help reduce your fears and understand the differences between rough-and-tumble play and rough play, here is a brief explanation of *rough play*. You should take action if you hear unhappy sounds and see children with sad- or angry-looking faces. If they appear to be frightened or hurting each other (hitting, kicking, or biting) as they physically interact, they are likely involved in rough play. If one child does not wish to continue the play or walks away and is not eager to return, you are probably observing rough play. With your supervision and the modeling of appropriate play interactions, these will not be any of the outcomes you see as children become happily involved in rough-and-tumble play.

Consider the following snapshots of what you might expect to see when three- and four-year-olds engage in lively physical play:

- Three-year-olds enjoy bonding during close, lively, animated fingerplays.
- Three-year-olds learn about pacing themselves (revving up or slowing down) as they interact during an activity such as chase.
- Three-year-olds have fun cooperating as they use their large muscles during group play, such as rolling big balls or shaking a parachute.
- Four-year-olds learn that fun physical interactions, even among loud and active boys, do not have to be violent.
- Four-year-olds develop empathy as they react to a stop signal when the play is not comfortable for everyone.
- Four-year-olds experiment with different strategies as they learn to read each other's body language during rough-and-tumble play.

Now let's look more closely at the types of interactions that might be happening in your classroom as preschoolers engage in lively, active play together.

Amanda, a young three-year-old, wakes up from her nap slightly grumpy. Before putting Amanda's shoes on her, the teacher holds her in her lap, smiles, then gently grabs and energetically wiggles each of Amanda's toes in turn as she playfully recites the lines from the fingerplay "This Little Piggy Went to Market." By the time Mrs. Salado tickles Amanda's baby toe and exclaims, "Wee-wee-wee, all the way home," they are both laughing. Then they give each other big, giggly, animated hugs!

During this socially stimulating physical interaction, a strong adult provides some gentle roughhousing with a young child. When Mrs. Salado and Amanda hug at the end of their fun activity, they are feeling close to one another and enthusiastically bond together. The stimulation and the close contact of the hug provide a wonderful social benefit of releasing the hormone oxytocin into the body, which helps the child feel loved.

In the designated rough-and-tumble play area, three-year-old Dove is happily jumping up and down on a floor mattress chanting, "Jump, jump, jump!" When she tires of this, she spins around and around, repeating, "Twirl, twirl, twirl." On another mattress, Euseph and Corbin, four-year-olds, face each other and jump up and down holding hands. When Euseph loudly yells, "Roar," he pulls downward on Corbin's hands and they fall down together in a heap of "roars." Then Corbin announces, "My turn." "Okay," responds Euseph.

Three-year-olds are still happy playing by themselves. They love amusing themselves with repetitive simple body movements, such as jumping, spinning, and dancing. Three-year-olds and four-year-olds seem to instinctively tune into their body movements and often add accompanying language to these rhythms. As they bond together, four-year-old best friends learn the important skill of reading each other's body language. For example, when Euseph pulls down on Corbin's hand, both children know to fall. This type of play socially and physically demonstrates the concept of cause and effect for the participants.

Rough-and-tumble play encourages the development of a sense of fairness, such as when Corbin requests that they take turns pulling downward. This also gives each child an opportunity to try out the roles of leader and follower. This noisy type of rough-and-tumble play, so enjoyed by loud and active four-year-old boys, is a wonderful way for them to learn that physical interactions do not have to be violent. It also allows boys to touch each other and have physical contact in socially acceptable ways, such as patting each other on the back after a satisfying play activity.

In a comfortable area of the classroom, three preschool boys spontaneously decide to have a friendly pillow fight with big, soft pillows. They experiment with different ways to hold the pillows (two handed or in the middle) as they good naturedly whack their opponents (never around the head). Brian jumps aside when he hears Richard behind him. Because Liam wears a leg brace, Richard is careful not to knock him over. Brian laughs loudly as he makes a curled ball out of his body to reduce the target, then tries to roll away from Liam's pillow whacks.

Preschoolers love to imitate the pillow fights their parents have with them at home. This type of time-honored horseplay allows preschoolers to test and practice a myriad of beneficial skills—social, emotional, physical, and cognitive. It releases a specific chemical called *brain-derived neurotrophic factor*, or BDNF, which stimulates growth in the brain that enhances memory, logic, and learning abilities.

This type of rough-and-tumble play aids participants in learning to anticipate one another's moves and become aware of unpredictable strategies. Preschoolers discover how to fine-tune their techniques and push the boundaries, depending on their sensitivity to what is happening around them. Socially, they become aware of what their playmates like or do not like. They learn to adjust their play depending on the needs of their fellow players (whether they might be younger, have a disability, or be more timid). The interactions help them explore risk-taking and creative behaviors. Best of all, this exciting, fun, child-initiated play among friends says "I like you!"

Outdoors at the top of the grassy hill, several preschool girls are playing an exhilarating game of chase that turns into tag. When the child designated as "It" gets near a participant, the chased child speeds up and sprints ahead. However, another player runs slowly, just daring to be caught, and gets tagged. At the bottom of the hill, six boys are playing tug-of-war with a jump rope. Each team of three pulls hard on the rope, until finally, one group goes over the line and they all fall down on top of each other laughing.

A favorite rough-and-tumble activity for girls is chase. They feel very accomplished socially while they pay close attention to one another's nonverbal cues and they are able to tag a runner with an open palm. They also learn about pacing. They discover that after going full speed awhile it is important to calm down a bit to regulate themselves. Both outdoor groups are experiencing the sense of give and take during play interactions. The chasers and

taggers are also experiencing rough-and-tumble play within the confines of playing by the rules and channeling their competitive energies.

Because it is raining outside, Mrs. Grossman moves the dry plastic wading pool indoors. All of the children eagerly and loudly fill the pool by crumpling newspaper and throwing it in. Then, a small group of four boys hop in. At first, they joyously roll around. Then they enthusiastically throw the paper balls at each other. Revving up, they engage in some play fighting without touching each other. First they try shadow boxing, then they add some make-believe karate kicks. Finally, in pairs, they kneel and try out their wrestling skills (no grabbing above the shoulders). After being tackled, Ryan yells, "Stop!" Then, catching his breath, he smiles and rejoins the kneeling wrestling activity.

When young children are pent up inside because of the weather, they need activities to help them expend their energy and release their stress. An experienced teacher, like Mrs. Grossman, knows how beneficial it is to encourage her preschoolers to explore gross motor activities in ways that don't involve hurting each other. Socially, it is fun for the entire class to cooperate on a simple project, such as using their big muscles to crumple up enough paper to fill the wading pool.

For the sake of safety, it is exciting for a few children, rather than a large group, to initiate big body play by incorporating fantasy play moves (such as karate chopping). Boys love to wrestle and hold each other down. It is part of learning how to read each other's reactions. They develop strategies by trial and error, such as learning how and where to grab another participant while being mindful of their opponent's comfort as well as their own strength. They develop empathy as they learn when to stop if interactions are not comfortable for everybody. The feeling of a connection with another person is a pleasant benefit to rough-and-tumble play.

What You Can Do

- **Provide a specific safe area for roughhousing.** Make sure there are soft landing places. Outside, rope off a grassy area for running or rolling down a hill. Pick up sharp sticks and stones. Inside, mark off boundaries for active play. Remove items with pointed corners and furniture that could be bumped into or toppled over. For wrestling and jumping, add a thick floor mat or old mattresses.

- **Create and enforce rules.** Limit the group size for safety and effective supervision. Select a special signal (such as yelling out "bubbles") that a child can use if she wants to get out of the rough-and-tumble play. Help her feel comfortable stopping and then returning. Model how to tap with an open hand, rather than to bump with a fist or push during tag.

- **Develop fun rough-and-tumble play activities.** Place them in a designated center where noise is allowed! Spontaneous activities can be part of regular free-choice play time. For example, supply empty clean plastic bottles to knock down with a ball or to kick around. Spread out plastic bubble-wrap sheets to jump on and pop. Provide a giant ball to push back and forth. Let children roll around in a huge box of Styrofoam packing squiggles.

- **Demonstrate and practice how to use specific materials safely.** For example, when children are involved in pillow fighting, make sure they understand that they are not allowed to hit anyone on the head or smother anyone. Use large, soft, fluffy pillows. Hold the zipper side and whack with the other side. Discuss whether to use one or two hands to swing the pillow.

- **Communicate the benefits to parents.** Parents are often nervous about rough-and-tumble play activities, but you can help them feel comfortable about this type of play and lend their support to your program. You can share safety rules and the benefits in a flyer or a handbook. Display positive, fun pictures on your parent bulletin board or website. Discuss a child's spirited participation during parent conferences. Encourage parent questions.

Other Aspects to Consider—Alerts

- **Watch out for play turning aggressive.** If you see unhappy faces or closed fists, rough play may be escalating. Get involved and stop or redirect the play. Discuss suitable ways to play in order to continue. Model appropriate techniques, such as using open hands instead of closed fists and not touching above the shoulders. Explain that rough-and-tumble play is not about winning, losing, or competition.
- **Be aware of bullying.** Some children are quite naturally loud, overly excited, and inclined to play hard. However, if a child seems to continually engage in excessive roughness and bully others, you may wish to talk with a therapist.
- **Note the influence of conflict-driven superheroes.** Sometimes, high-action fantasy play gets out of control. Remind the children that superheroes are helpful and rescue others as some of their goals. Brainstorm ways to tone down their physical interactions while championing their social causes.

Activities for Parents to Try at Home

- **Show children that safety is key.** Pair up children of the same size, similar age, and equal energy level. Explain that no hitting, pinching, or biting is allowed. No jumping from the furniture or the swing set is permitted. Have children take a break if negative behavior escalates. Let them cool off with a drink of water. Indoors, clear space to move around. Outside, use an area away from family activity, such as the picnic table.

- **Limit exposure to media violence.** While playing video games or watching movies or TV, your child observes superheroes and other characters solving their problems by kicking, hitting, and hurting others. Have a discussion about this type of roughness and the consequences.

- **Go slowly at first.** First, identify your comfort level with rough-and-tumble play. If you want to throw your child in the air or wrestle with him, be sure he is ready for your initiation of roughhousing and tumble play. His temperament will clue you in as to whether you should go full steam ahead or start out gently.

- **Learn some tickle activities.** Delightful tickling songs and fingerplays can provide a wonderful opportunity for bonding and lots of laughter. When I was young, Grandmother Anderson would take two fingers and walk them up my arm as she sang, "Creepy mouse, creepy mouse, tickle you right there!" And I would squeal with delight and anticipation, not knowing if the creepy mouse would tickle me under the chin or ribs. The bonding memory of this gentle rough-and-tumble play was so strong that years later I enjoyed doing this same activity with my preschoolers and my own son and grandsons!

- **Roughhouse with your daughter, too.** Boys seem to engage quite naturally in lively play activities. Studies show that boys account for 80 percent of rough-and-tumble play. Don't leave your girls out. Research implies that girls who interact with their dads show more confidence. Develop some fun moves such as chasing or dancing and falling down. Eliminate gender boundaries; invite Mom and Gram to join in. Dad and Grandpa shouldn't have all the fun!

Related Books to Read with Children

Barton, Chris. 2010. *Shark vs. Train*. New York: Little, Brown Books for Young Readers.

Morales, Yuyi. 2013. *Niño Wrestles the World*. New York: Roaring Brook Press.

Schmid, Sophie, and Sabine Praml. 2006. *One, Two, Three, Pull!* New York: North-South Books.

Sendak, Maurice. 1963. *Where the Wild Things Are*. New York: HarperCollins.

Wheeler, Lisa. 2004. *Bubble Gum, Bubble Gum*. New York: Little, Brown Books for Young Readers.

6

EXPLORING
DIVERSITY

Diversity—learning about others' unique qualities and respecting and accepting their differences; appreciating the scope of such things as race, ethnicity, religious beliefs, language, and traditions

aturally, the three- and four-year-olds in your classroom come from varied backgrounds, and their ability to appreciate those differences will also vary. Yet you are likely to see some of the following tendencies as children develop an awareness of diversity:

- Three-year-olds wonder where skin, eye, or hair color comes from.
- Three-year-olds hold perceptions that often appear distorted because they cannot see things from another's viewpoint.
- Three-year-olds react to the appearances of others.
- Four-year-olds begin to decenter and actively piece together their own identities by exploring others' similarities and differences.

- Four-year-olds imitate the way their families talk, and they feel that the way family members speak is the right way.
- Four-year-olds are beginning to identify with their own ethnic groups.

To get a better idea of how diversity might affect interactions among preschoolers in your care, let's explore some classroom scenarios.

Nora, a three-year-old, keeps looking at the new girl in the class. Nora has a puzzled look on her face. Her teacher, Mrs. Zuniga, asks, "What is the matter?" Nora says, "I think Shanice has a problem. She stayed in the sun too long. She got too tanned. She is very brown!" Mrs. Zuniga explains, "Don't worry. Shanice is fine. Her skin is supposed to be like that. She is naturally brown because she is an African American." Now, Nora looks even more bewildered. She replies, "I am an American. My skin doesn't look brown. It's white."

Nora's confusion and questions are typical of a preschooler's reaction to racial and cultural differences in others. Although preschoolers are quite curious about physical appearances in others, they are often more interested in their own. By age three or four, they are able to identify, label, and match others according to various racial characteristics, such as eye shape, hair texture, and skin color. Because color is an early visual category emphasized in preschool, it makes sense that skin color is noticed before other features, such as hair texture. Full of questions, three-year-olds often wonder where their skin, eye, or hair color comes from. They express some concern about whether their skin color will remain the same or change when they grow up. Still in a preoperational stage of their cognitive development, preschoolers attempt to figure out things around them as they organize information—such as size, gender, or skin color—into categories related to their own prior experiences.

Basing her thinking on what she has experienced, Nora finds inconsistencies in what her teacher is telling her. During the summer, Nora spent a lot of time swimming at the pool. She is quite aware that her skin became tanned and turned a brown color because of the sunshine. Then, during the winter, Nora noticed her skin turned back to white again. Nora wonders if this could happen to Shanice. It is difficult for Nora to comprehend that Shanice's

Social Development of Three- and Four-Year-Olds

skin color is permanent. Mrs. Zuniga has to explain, "Our skin color comes from melanin. We get melanin from our parents, and it is inside our bodies when we are born. This is why we can't change our skin color."

Three-year-olds, like Nora, are still operating from an egocentric base and relate their observations and ideas to themselves. Knowing that she is also an American, and white, it is hard for her to understand that African Americans are also called Black when Shanice looks brown. Nora's perceptions frequently appear distorted because she is not necessarily able to see things from another's point of view. Somewhere between the ages of three and five, preschoolers become aware of racial categories, although they do not always classify themselves accurately. By age four, they are tuned into the names given by society for various racial groups; however, they still may have a difficult time figuring out where they fit into the different classifications. Adult categories are confusing to preschoolers. For example, they wonder how it is possible for a dark-skinned child to have a light-skinned parent.

As they approach age four and a half, many preschoolers begin to decenter and become less egocentric. These preschoolers actively piece together their own identities by exploring how they are similar to and different from other people. Using his own family as an example, four-year-old Cameron explains to his teacher, "My sister has brown eyes, just like my mom. I have blue eyes, like my dad." This personal context helps Cameron understand that while his eyes are round, like his parents' eyes, Hong has almond-shaped eyes like his father, who is Chinese.

Some challenges can arise out of a lack of understanding. Max tells his teacher, Mr. Slivko, "I don't want to sit next to Tatsuo anymore. He smells like fish and talks funny." Tuned into his own way of doing things, Max feels that the way he speaks is the only right way. He is beginning to identify with his own ethnic group. Seeing himself as belonging to a family, he imitates the way his parents talk.

Although four-year-old Max may not exactly understand the concept of culture, he is aware of concrete differences in such things as clothing, languages, foods, and eating styles. Three-year-old Nora reacts to the appearance of others, and four-year-old Max also notices the way that people act, as he did with Tatsuo.

Sometimes, three- and four-year-olds appear to react unkindly or negatively to cultural differences that relate to ethnic identities that don't make sense to them. It is helpful for a knowledgeable teacher or parent to talk about these differences so they do not reject others because they are uncomfortable with a trait that is different. Max's teacher, Mr. Slivko explains, "Tatsuo speaks Japanese because that is the language his parents speak to him at home. Maybe we can ask Tatsuo if he will teach us a few words of Japanese, and then it won't seem strange to you. And Tatsuo smells like fish sometimes because his family enjoys special raw fish meals, called *sashimi*, the same way you love to eat your mom's spicy chili."

Young children often make generalizations, which may become stereotyped views of others. Just because a child might have seen a Hawaiian person wearing a grass skirt, she needs to be careful that she doesn't believe that all Hawaiians wear grass skirts.

Preschoolers are inclined to feel that if they try out a specific ethnic physical object, such as using chopsticks or dressing up in a sombrero, they could become a member of that cultural group. You can explain that culture comes from the people in your family and the way they were raised.

Celebrating family, national, and religious holidays is a cause for great excitement for young children. These events are wonderful times for three- and four-year-olds to learn in

natural ways from their peers and teachers about their diverse cultures through creating and eating various ethnic foods and engaging in dramatic play. For example, during the winter months, many cultural celebrations occur, such as African American Kwanzaa, East Indian Diwali, Christian Christmas, and Jewish Hanukkah. Although there may be differences in all of these holidays, young children can also find many similarities,

such as sharing special foods, decorating with lights, and participating in various family activities.

What You Can Do

- **Create graphs.** Discuss ways your preschoolers look different: hair length, hair color, hair texture, eye color, eye shape, and skin color. Then create human graphs by having children with similarities stand next to each other. Talk about how many of these traits come from their parents. How many belong to similar groups. Try other graphs, such as how many like to eat certain foods (such as sushi, flan, rugelach, and macaroni and cheese).

- **Use representational art materials.** Supply clay, paint, and crayons in a variety of skin tones so that children are able to draw or model themselves, their families, and their friends. Set out nonbreakable mirrors for children to use while drawing self-portraits. Add interesting collage materials so preschoolers can create a mural of children around the world.

- **Enhance your construction area.** Hang up travel posters and pictures of dwellings and famous structures from different places in the world. Provide blocks, boxes, and boards to construct and then play in these excitingly different buildings, such as a hogan or a tree house. Add figurines that represent a variety of racial and cultural backgrounds. Encourage the children to dramatize how they might play, live, and work in these structures. Add some animals and vehicles (carts or boats, maybe) from other settings.

- **Experience multicultural music.** Encourage parents and their children to share music and songs from their heritage either from a recording or during a live performance. Have them demonstrate cultural dances with appropriate accessories (such as scarves or wrist bells). Invite the preschoolers to join in. Provide interesting instruments for the children to explore, such as Tibetan bells, castanets, conch shell horns, and pan flutes.

- **Invite family members to contribute authentic items.** Ask relatives to share family recipes and come in to cook with the preschoolers, if they can. Ask them to lend the class some food-related items from their culture to use during dramatic play (such as a wok, chopsticks, or empty food boxes printed with their home language). Have a family member read a favorite book recorded in the home language for the children to enjoy in school.

OTHER ASPECTS TO CONSIDER—ALERTS

- **A child might echo another's prejudices and say something inappropriate.** If a young child doesn't understand something, he may observe another person's bias and react accordingly, which may appear disrespectful. For example, he might say, "You look funny wearing that scarf-thing when it's hot in the summer." Instead, help the child learn to ask a question in a more positive way, such as, "Why do you always wear that around your face?"

- **Notice if a child is describing people by using broad stereotypes.** Does she believe that all Native American people live in wigwams or all Hispanic people wear serapes? If so, she needs assistance to see how people of various cultures dress and live today.

- **A child may be upset with how another child responds to his body contact or variations in personal space.** Help the child see that not all cultures are comfortable with hugging or touching. In certain Asian cultures it is disrespectful for a child to make eye contact with an older person, such as the teacher. Usually children's differences follow actions that their parents are comfortable with, so they do not seem strange to them.

Activities for Parents to Try at Home

- **Teach how to be respectful.** Encourage your child to ask questions in positive ways. For example, "Why do you eat with your fingers?" instead of "You look messy pushing bread around on your plate." Explain, "Differences are natural, not wrong or bad. Your hair is a blond color; mine is brown." Listen to words of greeting in various languages so your child experiences and enjoys hearing different language patterns.
- **Feel comfortable with your own diversity.** Create a family album. Add family photos from the past and present. Write down or record favorite family stories. Draw pictures of special family traditions. Include traditional recipes.
- **Explore gardening and foods.** Outdoors or indoors in pots, try growing herbs such as cilantro, oregano, lemon grass, mint, basil, sage, and parsley. Introduce your child to new foods from other cultures by using these herbs as you cook. For example, you could make Mexican guacamole with cilantro, Italian pizza with basil, and Middle Eastern food with mint. Have a tasting party!

Related Books to Read with Children

Choi, Yangsook. 2001. *The Name Jar*. New York: Dell Dragonfly Books.

Fox, Mem. 2006. *Whoever You Are*. Boston: HMH Books for Young Readers.

Joosse, Barbara M. 1992. *Mama, Do You Love Me?* New York: Scholastic.

Simon, Norma. 1999. *All Kinds of Children*. Morton Grove, IL: Albert Whitman.

Tafolla, Carmen. 2009. *What Can You Do With a Paleta?/¿Qué Puedes Hacer con una Paleta?* (English and Spanish Edition). Berkeley, CA: Tricycle Press.

Tarpley, Natasha. 2003. *I Love My Hair*. Boston: Little, Brown.

Wells, Rosemary. 2009. *Yoko*. New York: Hyperion.

7

DEVELOPING GENDER AWARENESS

Gender awareness—gaining an understanding and knowledge of the differences in roles and relations between boys and girls

Three- and four-year-olds may have different ideas about stereotypical gender roles during play. During the preschool years, children develop a curiosity about private body parts and an understanding about their own sex and the stability of sex as they grow up into men and women. Although not all children develop at the same rate or achieve specific milestones at the same time, the following types of behaviors provide a glimpse into what you can probably expect to see as gender awareness develops:

- Three-year-olds can accurately label themselves and others as a boy or a girl.
- Three-year-olds are unconcerned if a boy plays with an item considered to be a girl's object, such as a purse.
- Three-year-olds may be uncertain whether a girl stays a girl or changes into a boy as she grows up.
- Four-year-olds can be judgmental and critical of cross-gender play activities.

- Four-year-olds are influenced by the idea that girls and girls' stuff are the opposite of boys and boys' stuff.
- Four-year-olds demonstrate a curiosity about private body parts.

Now let's look at some scenarios that will show how different levels of gender awareness might affect preschoolers' behavior in the classroom.

On the first day of preschool, three-year-old Avery introduces herself to Skylar, who is playing with a doll in the dramatic play center. She explains, "I'm Avery. I have a new baby sister. She is a girl like me."

Avery's introduction is not surprising. By two and half to three years of age, preschoolers are well aware of gender identity, that is, knowing whether they are girls or boys. Three-year-olds are able to accurately label themselves and others, as Avery did, as a girl or a boy. Also, at this age they know to use the appropriate common pronouns to label a girl as "she" and a boy as "he."

It is also not astonishing that Avery finds her new friend playing with a doll in the dramatic play center. Through dramatic play, children have an opportunity to explore and understand gender roles. As soon as young children are comfortably able to label themselves as a girl or a boy, they demonstrate a preference for gender-typed play activities. This indicates a social connection between gender identity formation and play. Children learn early on from their parents what is acceptable for each gender; therefore, sex roles and stereotypes are established. After observing her mom, Skylar plays with her doll, as she identifies with activities and occupations traditionally viewed as appropriate for girls. Skylar is imitating her mother's actions at home.

Like Skylar, who is involved in home and doll play, studies have shown that preschool girls tend to show a preference for art materials, symbolic activities, formal games, and dramatic play. Meanwhile, Carter and Henry are busy at the carpentry bench hammering nails into wood to create a kayak. Natural preferences for play materials and toys for boys tend to include working with structured materials, such as blocks, playing with wheeled vehicles, climbing on outdoor structures, and playing with sand. It is important for the classroom environment to reflect preschoolers' interests, which at times may be influenced by seemingly gender-stereotyped materials.

In another classroom, four-year-old Luke swaggers out of the dramatic play area swinging a huge purse that is holding his superhero character collection back and forth. Javier points and laughs. He says, "Hey, Luke, what's up with you? Only girls carry purses." Annoyed, Luke yells back, "I am a boy!"

Children's attitudes toward gender roles and activities are affected by their level of development. Most three-year-olds could not care less if Luke wished to play with a big mom-sized purse. As far as they are concerned, if it works for him as a container to carry his characters, that's okay. Four-year-olds are quite different, however; they prefer playing with friends of the same sex and are quite influenced by their choices of toys, accessories, and clothes. They can be rather judgmental and rigid. Preschool boys, like Javier, are apt to be critical of cross-gender play activities. For example, they feel that girls can diaper babies but not necessarily be firefighters. Or it's fine for a boy to be a ship's captain but not sew an outfit together—and certainly not carry a big purse!

About age four, preschoolers start to construct the concept that girls' stuff is the opposite of boys' stuff. They form inaccurate ideas, often suggested by their parents. They might embrace gender schemas that make assumptions, such as blue is for boys and therefore the blue tricycle is for boys. Unfortunately, toy manufacturers build on these expectations by designing pink beauty-salon play equipment targeted for little girls or blue baseball gloves created for little boys' hands.

Unsure of whether Charlie is actually a boy or a girl because he has very long curly hair, three-year-old Miko asks him, "Charlie, are you a boy?" Four-year-old Charlie responds, "Yes, I'm a boy. You are a girl. You are wearing a pretty barrette."

Preschoolers under four use their concrete thinking to help them determine their understanding of gender. Usually, they can focus on only one particular characteristic at a time. Like Miko, they look at aspects such as length of hair or behavior to judge gender. By four they are checking out clothing, accessories, and physical appearance as ways to distinguish gender identity.

When asked, "What will you be when you grow up, a man or a woman?" children who are older four-year-olds and up tend to answer the question with their own gender. At that age, children are able to coordinate two symbolic relationships. They understand that their gender will remain stable as they develop (unless they make a conscious choice to change it). Girls will grow up to become women, and boys will grow up to become men. However, younger children may be uncertain whether a boy stays a boy or changes into a girl as he grows up. Before preschoolers reach the gender-stability stage, their pretend play tends to embrace different gender roles as they act out situations. For instance, three-year-old Evan may decide to be the mother while eating a pretend meal with Carina; he has not yet reached the stage when he wants to affirm his gender role and identity as a boy.

Charlotte and Grayson, two older four-year-olds, are playing hospital in the medical center they have created. They are giggling as they try out various names for anatomical differences on their sick doll patients.

It is not at all uncommon for children of this age to demonstrate a curiosity about private body parts. By four, they are aware that anatomy differs between the sexes. However, they do not understand that the genitals are the one feature that distinguishes a man from a woman. This may not occur until age six. Like Miko and Charlie, they are strongly influenced by irrelevant, external factors (such as appearance and type of toy selected) when trying to identify gender.

A group of four-year-old boys spend all morning engineering a magnificent, huge fort by combining the hollow blocks and the wooden blocks with the large chunks of plastic pipes. When Miranda asks if she can help with the building, the boys yell in unison, "No girls allowed!" Upset, Miranda asks, "Why not?" The boys respond, "Because you are not strong enough. Girls are weak."

With gender exclusion and gender-role inflexibility, these preschoolers are learning to focus on gender cues they have probably heard from their peers, parents, teachers, and media, such as in TV programs and in video games. These stereotypical mixed messages from their environment, culture, and media sometimes encourage them to react with negative behaviors. Their reactions may be related to hearing little girls being praised for being pretty, neat, and helpful; whereas, little boys are seen as being noisy and action-oriented. Boys often receive encouragement for their sense of adventure and physical skills. Boys and girls discover in their preschool years that they are treated differently through gender-stereotyped activities and toys.

Mrs. Muson notices in her preschool classroom that the girls are apt to naturally be drawn to traditional girl activities with their female friends, such as cooking, drawing, and rearranging the kitchen area. The boys gravitate toward things of interest to males with their boy peers, such as driving vehicles in the construction center and roughhousing in the ball pit. Knowing that these gender-role behaviors and same-sex play are normal and that the children will usually choose these activities, Mrs. Muson wants to take her classroom in a slightly different direction. She decides to move the dramatic play center next to the block area to stimulate cross-gender play.

With the addition of interesting props, the preschoolers in her classroom delight in using their imaginations to create activities that appeal to both sexes, such as a grocery store and a shoe and hat shop, just like at the mall. When boys and girls are encouraged to work together as designers and problem solvers with materials of interest to both, some of the negative gender stereotypes fade away as play develops in a more nonsexist manner.

What You Can Do

- **Create environments that can be enjoyed by both sexes.** Entice boys to the art center by adding mallets to clay play or boosting the appeal of clay with small dinosaur models. Encourage girls to explore the block center with the addition of some family figurines. Offer gender-neutral types of materials, such as placing a wide variety of fabric in the dramatic play area. Children might pretend the fabric is a picnic cloth, a cape, a baby blanket, a tent, and many more creative ideas.
- **Offer activities to promote collaboration between boys and girls.** Encourage a small group of boys and girls to focus on a specific goal and integrate each other's ideas. Try cooperating to put together a big puzzle or create peanut butter pinecone bird feeders, for example.
- **Help children see that both sexes can have a variety of careers.** Share posters of a woman and a man performing the same job, such as a nurse or police officer. Invite parents to share information about their jobs. When I taught preschool, a child's mom brought in her equipment to demonstrate her occupation as a beekeeper. Both girls and boys enjoyed her presentation, and they got to eat the yummy honey for snack!
- **Expose children to unbiased books.** Share stories that provide empowered images of characters with positive self-images and anti-bias attitudes. Help children evaluate books for gender stereotypes.
- **Be aware of your attitude.** Make sure the messages you share are not stereotyped, but support your children's roles and activities as they develop who they are. For instance, do you say that "big boys don't cry"? Do you refer to little girls as "honey" or "sweetie" and comment on how pretty they look in their cute dresses?

OTHER ASPECTS TO CONSIDER—ALERTS

- **It is not all right to exclude others.** It is natural that children enjoy playing with their special same-sex friends or may not wish to add another child to a group activity, but if you find that certain children seem to make a habit of excluding others based on their gender, this needs to be addressed. With shouts of "Girls stay out. Boys only!" feelings are bound to be hurt, and those discriminated against may suffer from a sense of unfairness.

- **Are you apt to reinforce only what children do well?** Do you play to boys' and girls' strengths instead of encouraging an environment that also improves their weaknesses? Children are inclined to participate in activities that they are proficient in; therefore, girls might not be as apt to select activities involving gross motor or spatial skills. Boys may not choose activities that feature listening skills, which boys tend to develop more slowly than girls.

- **Does a child need a positive role model?** A particular child may live in a situation with a single parent because of divorce, death, deployment, or other circumstances. It might be of great benefit for this child to spend some quality time with a person of the absent sex. With the parent's consent, work with social services or agencies such as foster grandparents or college volunteers to find an appropriate match to help the child strengthen gender and role awareness.

ACTIVITIES FOR PARENTS TO TRY AT HOME

- **Be approachable.** When your child expresses curiosity about anatomy and sexuality, don't be shocked or embarrassed. This interest is natural. Keep your communication very simple. Your child isn't looking for a long, technical explanation. Preschoolers need help in understanding that their bodies (not their clothes or choice of toys) determine their sex.

- **Take note of chore assignments.** Children learn to link certain types of household chores by gender. They may think that males tend to handle outdoor maintenance types of chores, such as lawn mowing, and that females tend to perform more jobs inside the home, such as

laundry. It is normal that your son will want to do things like his daddy. However, make sure your son has a chance to cook as well and that your daughter has an opportunity to help with some home repairs.

- **Be aware of heavily gender-stereotyped consumer products.** Manufacturers place gender-typed messages on sheets and towels, clothes, toys, furniture, and even Band-Aids! These items are also merchandized in stores by aisles separated by gender. This may discourage children from purchasing and trying out products perceived as being only appropriate for a specific gender.

- **Evaluate TV programs together.** Often, children's television program characters are portrayed by action-oriented, tough male personalities and silly, helpless females. Discuss ways these stereotyped male characters might solve problems in more peaceful ways. How could the feminine characters take on stronger roles?

- **Create a scrapbook.** Take photos of your family throughout the week. Show traditional roles that help build your child's gender awareness, such as Mom cooking dinner and Dad tuning up the car engine. But also show photos of the whole family taking on other roles as well while camping—children setting the picnic table, then gathering firewood; Dad cooking hot dogs over the fire while Mom fishes.

RELATED BOOKS TO READ WITH CHILDREN

Fox, Mem. 1994. *Tough Boris.* San Diego: Harcourt Brace.

Hoffman, Mary. 1991. *Amazing Grace.* New York: Dial Books for Young Readers.

Leaf, Munro. 1936. *The Story of Ferdinand.* New York: Viking Press.

Rotner, Shelley. 1996. *Lots of Moms.* New York: Dial Books for Young Readers.

Spinelli, Eileen. 1993. *Boy, Can He Dance!* New York: Four Winds Press.

Waber, Bernard. 1973. *Ira Sleeps Over.* Boston: Houghton Mifflin.

DEVELOPING ACTIVE
LISTENING SKILLS

Active listening—concentrating on spoken words in an effort to understand and retain the message

Three- and four-year-olds are developing their ability to listen well, identify verbal patterns, and follow directions. They enjoy repetition, predictability, and silly play that revolves around words. You may notice some of the following tendencies as preschoolers' active listening skills develop:

- Three-year-olds love listening to and reciting nursery rhymes.
- Three-year-olds discover that various words begin with the same sound.
- Three-year-olds like to listen to favorite stories again and again to help them rehearse certain words to reread.
- Four-year-olds enjoy making up funny rhyming words to describe each other.
- Four-year-olds are surprised to discover that although some words sound the same, they have different meanings.

■ Four-year-olds become quite involved listening to each other's ideas and suggestions while solving problems together.

Now consider some more-detailed scenarios showing interactions you might see in your classroom.

Ashley and Brittany curl up on the couch with Ms. Kimble, the teacher of the three-year-old group, as she shares a nursery rhyme book with them. They have the most wonderful time repeating the rhymes to their teacher in singsong voices. Animatedly, the girls recite, "Little Bo-Peep has lost her sheep!"

Three-year-olds also enjoy playing with the words in their favorite songs. They listen to each other and giggle as they change the rhymes around to make funny verses. Bryce entertains Megan, and she eagerly listens while he sings, "Here we go looby loo, here we go pooby poo, here we go booby boo, all on a Saturday night."

Language is becoming fun for three-year-olds, who are developing quite an ear for different sounds as they listen to and repeat nursery rhymes, songs, and finger-plays. These activities all provide excellent opportunities for them to become aware of predictable rhymes and sound patterns. Three-year-olds love creating their own rhymes and silly words as they contrive how to manipulate and change words. They are also discovering that various words begin with the same sound, such as the /m/ in *Megan* and *Mommy*.

With preschoolers' ever-expanding cognitive and listening abilities, many children are able to understand 300 to 500 words by three years of age, depending on their experiences at home and in the community. By the time they are four years old, children tend to be aware of 1,500 to 2,500 words. At the end of their fourth year, they may have added an understanding of another 2,000 words. Many preschoolers add an average of four to six words daily to their receptive vocabularies.

Besides playing around repeating songs and rhymes, four-year-olds love to listen to each other's funny jokes and riddles (even if they frequently don't understand them). Damien listens intently when his buddy Shaquil asks, "What happens when Superman throws his alarm clock out of the window?" Damien shrugs his shoulders, then roars with laughter when Shaquil responds, "He makes time fly!" Noted for displaying an outrageous sense of humor, four-year-olds can be observed fooling around and listening to each other's preposterously silly banter throughout the day. For example, two girls take turns making up wacky rhyming words describing each other. Gayle and Patrice giggle when Gayle calls out, "Patrice is a funny, stuffy, fluffy, puffy!" Because they are still feeling silly later at the art table, they call the playdough "picky, icky, sticky stuff."

With their keenly developing listening and cognitive skills, four-year-olds are amazed when they realize that although some words may sound the same, they may quite well have different meanings. Jerrell's teacher asks him if he can help her find the mouse. Jerrell gets down on all fours and begins to make squeaking sounds as he looks around. His teacher begins to laugh as she holds up a digital mouse from behind another nearby computer. Together they enjoy the joke about the two very different things that have the same name.

In the literacy center, Angel enthusiastically requests, "Again, again!" These are words that you have undoubtedly heard many times after reading a favorite story to eager three-year-olds. After actively listening to *Goodnight Moon* by Margaret Wise Brown, Angel wants to hear Miss Caroline read the delightful rhyming phrases "Goodnight room," "Goodnight moon," and "Goodnight light / And the red balloon" again. Three-year-olds love hearing the same stories over and over. The repetition helps them rehearse particular words and repeat specific lines as they learn to help their teacher reread their favorite stories. Listening and rereading the words also helps them to increase their memory skills. Preschoolers love to listen to each other discussing their favorite stories. This is yet another important way to increase their vocabularies. Three-year-olds are now able to identify vocal changes when another person is speaking or reading.

In the art center, four-year-old Remy delights in drawing airplanes with markers. His teacher asks him to dictate a story about his interesting artwork. When she reads Remy's original story back to him, he listens very closely. This practice certainly enhances his receptive listening process.

Another wonderful way for young children to enrich their listening skills is through the give-and-take of conversations. For example, while playing in the dramatic play center, three-year-old Adam asks his pretend kitty, Willis, "What do you want to eat?" Adam

Social Development of Three- and Four-Year-Olds

listens carefully while Willis responds, "Fish and peanut butter cookies. Meow!" Adam tells Willis, "Stupid kitty. Cookies will make you sick. I get you fish at the store." Three-year-olds, like Adam, are able to add details to their conversations. They frequently ask and answer their own questions while they play. They quite enjoy hearing themselves talk or listening to their unique conversations with their special pretend characters.

By the time they reach age four, preschoolers are actively engaged with talking with their friends. For instance, Robin and Malena discuss the best way to water the outdoor vegetable garden. Robin suggests using the hose because it would be a fast way to water. However, Malena thinks it would be more fun to try sprinkling with the watering can. Four-year-olds become quite involved listening to each other's ideas and suggestions while working to solve problems. Sometimes their dialogues become very lengthy as they begin to understand the importance of using their receptive powers to listen to others in order to obtain information.

During snack, Ms. Scott says to Tabitha, "Please go under the table and pick up your napkin." Smiling, three-year-old Tabitha is pleased to comply with her teacher's request. Three-year-olds, like Tabitha, are easily able to actively listen to and respond to two-part directions. They are also able to listen to and follow directional commands, such as *beside, over,* and *through.*

Four-year-olds enjoy showing off that they can meet the challenge of successfully completing a set of three-step directions that they have been given. Two submariners create a sub with a large rectangular cardboard box on its side and a periscope made from a paper towel tube. Ibrahim, the captain of the submarine, gives Nolan, a sailor, a series of orders: "Make the periscope go down. Fasten the hatch. Quick, put the sub into a dive!" Nolan enthusiastically makes a loud siren sound as he goes through all of the required steps to get the submarine under water fast. Mission accomplished!

When preschoolers have more fully developed their active listening skills, they are able to focus their bodies and eyes on the person speaking while giving her their attention. As long as there aren't other distractions in the immediate environment, such as loud music or friends running nearby, they should be able to pay attention and listen.

On the other hand, while preschoolers are busy enhancing their own listening skills, they soon discover that others may not be listening attentively to them. They may not be focusing directly on them, may be looking elsewhere, or may be doing various tasks. It is quickly apparent to preschoolers if adults or peers are involved with other children or distracted by another project. Rather insistent, four-year-olds can be very demanding. Still quite self-centered, they want the other person's full attention. If they feel annoyed that the listener is not focusing on what they have to say, they will definitely question, "Are you listening to me?"

During their preschool years, young children, like Bryce, delight in displaying their language skills by changing word sounds all around. They also enjoy listening to rhyming patterns, as Ashley and Brittany did. They are starting to identify beginning and ending sounds in words. This process is all part of phonological awareness, a specialized type of listening skill that is necessary for children to begin to learn in order to eventually read. Having fun playing around with stories and listening to rhymes and riddles is a wonderful way to start your preschoolers off on their reading careers with exciting phonological awareness activities.

What You Can Do

- **Play listening games.** Enhance preschoolers' receptive listening skills. Tape familiar sounds in the environment (such as water flushing, a vacuum cleaner running, or scissors cutting paper). Have children listen, then guess what is making the sound. Clap simple patterns (such as two loud, two soft). Can the children duplicate what they just heard?

- **Incorporate splendid story sounds.** Encourage children to help you retell a story with sound effects (they could mimic a dog barking or a door creaking) and appropriate characters' voices (such as a babbling baby or a gruff pirate). Let the story listeners fill in anticipated words or phrases (such as "I'll huff and puff").

- **Use transition time.** Help children make transitions throughout the day by listening to and responding to various sounds or patterns. Ring a bell once to come to circle time. Use a series of three bell rings for cleanup. Use a particular beat pattern on a bongo drum to alert children to line up to go out to play.

- **Encourage students to be listening partners.** Provide comfortable, quiet spots in the classroom for pairs of children to chat with each other. After they listen to what their partners have to say, encourage them to select a special word or phrase about the conversation ("fluffy bunny") to share or maybe draw a picture about.

■ **Ask, "Did you mean that?"** Show your preschoolers that even when you are a good listener you can still get some funny results. Tell the children you will listen to and then follow their directions exactly. For example, they could explain how to create a peanut butter and jelly sandwich. If they say, "Spread the bread with peanut butter," spread both sides of a slice with peanut butter. How silly! Is that what they really meant?

OTHER ASPECTS TO CONSIDER—ALERTS

■ **Does the child seem not to comprehend what he hears?** Does he appear not to listen to you on a regular basis? His listening abilities may be temporarily compromised by an illness, an allergy, or a head cold. His hearing and listening skills could be affected by medical or development reasons that have more permanent consequences. Ask parents to share their observations of how well the child listens at home. The child may benefit from an assessment by a speech language pathologist or an evaluation by an audiologist.

■ **Do you find yourself repeating information to a certain child?** Does she appear interested in what you are saying? Is she focused? Is she involved with another activity instead of paying attention? Does she verbally respond? You may wish to consider checking for her dominant learning style. She may respond well to visual or kinesthetic stimulation, but simply not be an auditory learner.

■ **Consider the environment for a child identified with hearing impairments.** For example, if a child wears a hearing aide, this may make background noises appear quite loud. It may make it hard for the child to sort out information when he tries to listen. Help filter out loud sounds by strategically placing rugs and drapes to improve the acoustics in the room. Look at center placements—make sure quiet areas (such as the book corner) are not placed next to noisy areas (such as the block center). Place the child near you during circle and story times.

ACTIVITIES FOR PARENTS TO TRY AT HOME

■ **Demonstrate good listening skills.** If possible, situate yourself at your child's level during conversations. Make good eye contact. Be patient and don't interrupt. Focus on what she's saying. When responding, try not to speak too loudly or softly. Try not to fidget. Be attentive.

■ **Eliminate distracters.** Turn off or move away from the television. Don't talk on the phone or text while trying to listen to your child. Stop what you are doing if possible and concentrate on what your child is saying. If he is listening to you, have him look at you and focus by not bouncing his ball or watching his iPad.

- **Have a family sing-a-long.** Sing songs that require the singers to listen carefully, then follow the directions and act them out. Sing songs such as "The Hokey Pokey," "Where Is Thumbkin," and "Itsy Bitsy Spider." Enjoy singing songs with repeating sounds, such as "Bingo," or rhyming words, such as "This Old Man."

- **Follow along.** A great game to see if your child can listen and follow directions is, of course, "Simon Says." When the leader uses "Simon says" in the instructions, she must follow along. If the leader simply gives a command without using "Simon says" and the child follows it, then she must sit down! Have fun moving around as you sing, "follow the leader and clap your hands . . . stamp your feet . . . tap your knees. . . ." Let your child be the leader too.
- **Share silly sounds.** Have a contest. How many words can you say to rhyme with lake? Your child might say make, take, rake, or bake. It's okay if they don't make sense. Try out some old-time tongue twisters such as "She sells seashells down by the sea shore." Can your child say it faster?

RELATED BOOKS TO READ WITH CHILDREN

Binkhow, Howard. 2006. *Howard B. Wigglebottom Learns to Listen.* Marina del Rey, CA: Thunderbolt.

Brown, Margaret Wise. 2007. *Goodnight Moon.* New York: Harper & Row.

Martin, Bill, Jr. 1997. *Polar Bear, Polar Bear, What Do You Hear?* New York: Henry Holt.

Showers, Paul. 1993. *The Listening Walk.* New York: HarperCollins.

Stein, David Ezra. 2010. *Interrupting Chicken.* Somerville, MA: Candlewick Press.

Vallat, Christelle. 2014. *Celia.* White Plains, NY: Peter Pauper Press.

BUILDING **VERBAL COMMUNICATION SKILLS**

Verbal communication—expressive language transmitted with words and sound

Three- and four-year-olds enjoy playing with words and repeating silly phrases as they improve their vocabulary and conversation skills. Although they will not all achieve milestones at the same time, take a glimpse at what you might expect while preschoolers are developing their verbal communication skills:

- Children tend to be able to speak at least 300 words by age three.
- Three-year-olds may use the simple-past-tense rule for irregular-past-tense verbs (for example, saying *drawed* instead of *drew*).
- Three-year-olds may create a word if they are not sure of the precise term (such as a *picker-upper* for a *magnet*).
- A child's vocabulary tends to expand to at least 4,000 words by the end of the fourth year.

- Four-year-olds can master most pronouns, words for colors, and words for body parts, and can carry on an authentic conversation.
- Four-year-olds are noted for using silly or profane language to try to shock others.

Now let's explore in more detail some of the ways that children in your classroom might be interacting with you and each other while developing their verbal communication skills.

Four-year-old Ethan points to Kimee, the class fish. He asks his teacher, "What color is our fish?" Ms. Ryan replies, "Kimee is called a goldfish. What color do you think she is, Ethan?" "Oh! Gold, gold, gold—gold, gold!" Ethan responds in a delightful singsong voice. "Yes, our fish Kimee is gold," answers Ms. Ryan. Curious and full of questions, Ethan wants to know, "How can I turn gold? What if I swim in water? Will I turn gold?"

When preschoolers like Ethan use their expressive verbal language skills to share their feelings, ideas, and needs with others, it is such an important step toward interacting with those around them. With practice, the preschoolers' verbal communication and social skills develop a strong partnership.

Talking continuously to themselves, as well as others, preschoolers enjoy playing with words. Like Ethan, they ask countless questions just to keep communication open. During these years, their expressive language expands from about 300 words at age three to more than 4,000 words by the time they reach age five. Using language rules in natural ways, three-year-olds can usually comfortably speak with three or four words in a sentence, and four-year-olds tend to clearly communicate with four or more words in a sentence, such as when Ethan wondered aloud, "How can I turn gold?"

On the rug in Mrs. Tozier's class, three-year-olds gather around as she reads them a favorite funny book, *There Was an Old Monster* by Rebecca Emberley, Adrian Emberley, and Ed Emberley. They giggle as he swallows a tick that makes him sick. When Mrs. Tozier finishes the book, she asks, "Who can tell me what happened in the story?" Eva calls out, "Me can tell. Ants in his pants. He danced." The three-year-olds roar with laughter as they imitate and chant the silly repeating phrase "Scratchy, scratch."

Three-year-olds truly enjoy having books read to them. Reading is a wonderful activity to introduce them to a variety of concepts and new vocabulary words. They love rhymes such as *tick* and *sick* and delight in making up new rhymes. For instance, the three-year-olds decided to get rid of the tick by hitting it with a stick! They are able to retell stories and recall key events in order. Although three-year-olds may leave out a few details of a story, referring to the book's illustrations can be a helpful reminder of certain highlights.

When children reach age three, you should be able to understand at least 75 percent of what they say. A child of that age can usually tell you her own name and what street she lives on. She can use most pronouns correctly, but like Eva, may still be a little confused by *I* and *me*. It is rather common for a three-year-old to use the simple-past-tense rule for irregular-past-tense verbs. For example, she might say, "I *sitted* down on the chair" instead of *sat*.

In Mr. Bennett's class, the four-year-olds regularly visit the local library for story time. One day, they find a huge surprise hanging on the chain link fence outside of the library's side door. They discover sequential laminated pages of the book *Mike Mulligan and His Steam Shovel* right next to where the construction is under way for Middlebury's new town office building. Very excited, the children quickly recognize that the illustrations in Virginia Lee Burton's book and the words about construction activities in Popperville relate to what is happening in their very own town!

Using books as a springboard is a great way to introduce preschoolers to a whole new technical vocabulary, which helps them understand words in context and associate an activity with a group of words. Back at school, the class rereads the story. Then outside in the sandbox, the four-year-olds hold conversations about the toys they are using as props: a red steam shovel, a yellow backhoe, and a green digger. Acting out adult roles, they are clearly practicing using sentences with verbs about actions. For instance, Blair says, "I'm pulling back on the handle with my hand. Now the bucket picks up the dirt." Aaron eagerly continues the conversation, adding words that show his emotions. "I'm so excited. This is awesome. Our hole will be huge." By age five, children tend to have mastered most pronouns, words for colors, and words for body parts. Preschoolers can easily carry on an authentic conversation with their peers as well as adults.

In the dramatic play center, Brianna pretends to be a hair stylist, while Felicity acts as her customer in what the three-year-olds call the Sparkly Hair Salon. "What color do you want?" Brianna asks her client. "Brown," says Felicity. Brianna sprinkles make-believe hair color from a bottle. "Where is my dryer?" wonders Brianna. Felicity laughs, then points out, "Under the table." The appliances in the center all have the cords removed for safety. Brianna aims the dryer at Felicity's hair and makes a "rah" noise for the dryer. Not sure of what to call the curling iron, Brianna says, "I'm using the twirler thing." She then holds up a mirror and asks Felicity, "What do you think?" Felicity smiles, "Now I look beautiful!"

Three-year-olds, like Brianna and Felicity, really love to become involved with complicated plots with lots of back-and-forth dialogue. Adding toys and props to their dramatic play enhances their vocabularies and allows them to practice and build their communication skills. They enjoy asking questions that begin with words such as *what*, *where*, *who*, *when*, and *how*. Three-year-olds comfortably use simple prepositions in their conversations. And, they feel confident enough to create a word if they aren't sure of it, like Brianna's *twirler*.

After a trip to the farm, the children in Miss Heather's four-year-olds class describe what they saw there. Jade relates, "We helped put out corn for the chickens." Hunter raises his hand to add something. "This morning I put water in my dog's bowl. Then he spilled it!" Miss Heather thanks Hunter for raising his hand to take his turn talking but gently reminds him, "Hunter, the class is discussing their farm trip right now."

Four-year-olds are becoming more skilled in initiating conversations. They often open up with "Guess what?" or "You know. . . ." Sometimes, they simply try to grab your attention with "Hey!" They are less likely to interrupt the current speaker than when they were three, but they would really like a chance to talk after each speaker if they could. However, like Hunter, they frequently wish to use their turn to describe personal information, rather than stick to the topic at hand.

Preschoolers have a fabulous time playing with language. Three-year-olds love making up funny rhymes, such as calling a friend "Bobby-wobby" or reciting rhyming songs or nursery rhymes, such as "One, two, buckle my shoe." Four-year-olds adore repeating alliterations and amusing tongue twisters, such as "Peter Piper picked a peck of pickled peppers." Then they howl with laughter as they go faster each time and mess up saying the words. However, four-year-olds are noted for using silly or profane language to try to shock their buddies. For example, while constructing a wooden car at the workbench, Danny grins as he tells his friend Michael, "When you hit your thumb with the hammer, it is called a *damn-it*." Can you guess where Danny heard that?

Social Development of Three- and Four-Year-Olds

You might have fun listening to this goofy four-year-old riddle. Question: "What is black and white and red all over?" Answer: "An embarrassed zebra." It's a guarantee—four-year-olds will laugh hysterically whether they understand the answer or not!

WHAT YOU CAN DO

- **Support conversations with prop boxes.** Ask parents to contribute materials, such as baby items, walkie-talkies, and office supplies, to use for dramatic play. Group the materials in see-through plastic storage boxes with lids, so the preschoolers can use the materials independently to create interesting dialogues with their play.

- **Develop themes based on children's interests.** Observe their conversations, then provide related items to capitalize on their ideas. Allow time for concepts and vocabulary to develop. Children (especially those who speak English as a second language) will not have rehearsal time if themes are changed too quickly. For example, you might provide empty food boxes and a cash register for a supermarket theme. Or add miniature animals and people to the table blocks for a veterinarian theme.

- **Show and tell with a twist.** Provide a special corner in the classroom that promotes interesting conversations. When a child has something to share from home (such as a bird's nest, favorite seashell, or birthday present from Grandma), encourage several of his buddies to gather around while he describes the item. Then invite his peers to ask questions. Be sure they know that their ways of verbally expressing themselves will be valued.

- **Make up dialogue for wordless picture books.** My preschoolers loved this activity! Our favorite books were *The Snowman* by Raymond Briggs and *Changes, Changes* by Pat Hutchins. The children would use the pictures to predict what might happen next. They discussed descriptive words for their own feelings or about the illustrated actions. Then I wrote the serious, talented, young authors' dialogues on sticky notes. Next, I attached them to the appropriate wordless picture pages. Finally, we read and reread the book, sometimes adding an extra sticky note with their fresh ideas. Such fun!

- **Play lots of language games.** Offer the children many ways to express themselves verbally. Play a game based on categories: ask them to describe as many ice cream flavors or pizza toppings as they can think of. Pick a child's name, such as Bryan, and discuss words that begin like the beginning sound in his name—book, ball, and bounce. If they need a bigger challenge, ask them to shout out words that end like the ending sound in Bryan, such as fan and tan. Enjoy a silly riddle or joke festival!

Other Aspects to Consider—Alerts

- **Preschoolers can be overwhelmed with responding.** Three-year-olds often don't know what to say, so they simply shrug, giggle, or mumble "OK" if asked a question. Some young children have difficulty knowing when or how to enter a conversation. Instead of assuming they have a lag in language development, guide them to understand different signals that let them know when it is their turn to speak. For instance, when a speaker's voice tone changes or a person stops talking, it is their time to say something. Try coaching pairs to practice turn-taking before having children take turns speaking in a more overwhelming group setting.

- **Some children experience an articulation delay.** A child may have an oral-motor problem that relates to his ability to create certain sounds. Or a child may have difficulty with word retrieval. This indicates he has problems determining the words for what he wishes to say. It is possible that the preschooler might have questions about planning and sequencing a conversation. The American Speech-Language-Hearing Association suggests that parents contact a licensed speech-language pathologist to respond to their concerns and evaluate their child.

- **Dual language learners may need additional support.** Use short sentences and model conversation skills. Make vocabulary lists related to themes you are investigating. Explore a theme for several days so the child has an opportunity to practice new words. Share books written in English and the child's home language, such as the English-Spanish book *Oh, the Colors/De Colores* by Ashley Wolff, which features a traditional Spanish folk song. Help the dual language learner feel comfortable by using the correct pronunciation for her name and asking her to teach the class words in her home language.

Activities for Parents to Try at Home

- **Introduce new vocabulary during daily routines.** At meal time, describe new foods, such as squiggly pasta and sour cream topping. Use size, number, and color words in descriptions while your child gets dressed, such as two gigantic buttons and your fluffy, pink dress. You might use specialized words while cooking or folding laundry together, such as a pint basket of berries or a pair of socks.

- **Create original stories.** After your child has drawn a picture, invite her to dictate her own words about her drawing so you can write them down. Read her story together. Share conversations about her work (why she used a red line across the top or where her cat in the picture is going). Provide interesting collage materials, such as feathers, ribbons, foil, and glue, so she can create story starters.

- **Decorate talking heads.** Together, use socks, paper bags, or paper plates along with markers, yarn, and glue to design whimsical puppets. Have fun creating conversations for the imaginative characters. Maybe you can help your child stage a hit Broadway play from behind the couch to entertain the rest of the family.

- **Engage in fun language activities.** Play an old favorite guessing game. While taking turns saying "I spy with my little eye . . . ," use descriptive words, such as something green or something round. Provide two phones to practice exciting authentic conversations between the caller and receiver. Get physical and encourage your child to move to action words. Ask him to "jump like a. . . ." Then have him provide a verbal and physical response, such as a kangaroo or rabbit. Ask him to describe the animal after doing the action and saying the word.

- **Take brief field trips to jump-start conversations.** On trips to the park, pizza parlor, car wash, or library, take photos to review later and talk about what you saw and did. Write down highlighted new vocabulary words—such as *bristles*, *spray*, and *water pressure* for the car wash—and post them under a trip picture. Add new words after each trip to build up a personalized dictionary page.

RELATED BOOKS TO READ WITH CHILDREN

Briggs, Raymond. 1978. *The Snowman*. New York: Random House.

Cook, Julia. 2006. *My Mouth Is a Volcano*. Chattanooga, TN: National Center for Youth Issues.

Dunklee, Annika. 2011. *My Name Is Elizabeth!* Toronto: Kids Can Press.

Henkes, Kevin. 2010. *Wemberly Worried*. New York: Greenwillow Books.

Hutchins, Pat. 1971. *Changes, Changes*. New York: Macmillan.

Reid, Margarette S. 1997. *A String of Beads*. New York: Dutton Children's Books.

Wells, Rosemary. 2015. *Use Your Words, Sophie!* New York: Viking Books for Young Readers.

Wolff, Ashley. 2003. *Oh, the Colors: Sing Along in English and Spanish!/¡De Colores: Vamos a cantar junto en Inglés y Español!* Boston: Little, Brown.

Zolotow, Charlotte. 1999. *Some Things Go Together*. New York: HarperFestival.

10

PARTICIPATING IN
IMAGINATIVE PLAY

Imaginative play—activities that encourage children to invent different pretend scenarios from their minds, then act them out in various ways

Although imaginative play is open-ended and tends to reflect snippets of the unique experiences each child has, you will notice some common tendencies among three- and four-year-olds as they engage in these creative activities:

- Three-year-olds frequently notice another child's play behavior, then copy it.
- Three-year-olds are often fixated on a particular prop.
- Three-year-olds freely switch from one pretend play role to another.
- Four-year-olds add complexity and depth to their imaginative play with their choice of props and accessories.
- Four-year-olds, especially boys, love to participate in noisy, active pretend play with their peers.
- Four-year-olds enjoy sharing ideas with others and incorporating them during imaginative cooperative play.

The following scenarios will give you more insight into how preschoolers tend to interact during pretend play and will highlight some of the types of imaginative activities you might see in your classroom.

In the dramatic play center, young three-year-olds Ariel and Lisa are pretending to be mommies as they both play with baby dolls. Ariel rocks her sick baby and sings to her, "Get better soon." Lisa feeds her baby doll a bottle, and then burps her by patting her back. She observes how Ariel rocks her baby. Lisa mimics this comforting action, and then wraps her baby in a soft blanket so she'll go to sleep. Next, she leaves her napping baby to go and cook pancakes on the stove in the kitchen play area.

Frequently, you see two young three-year-olds, like Ariel and Lisa, sit next to each other as they enjoy playing with similar materials. According to child development researcher Mildred Parten, in this type of parallel play children may appear to have little actual social contact with each other; however, they often notice the other child's behavior and copy it.

Three-year-olds' imaginative play is commonly based on experiences they have had or witnessed, such as the way Ariel's and Lisa's mommies care for younger siblings at home. They enjoy mimicking these real-life experiences and reenacting daily routines in their imaginative play. Acting out family and domestic themes, three-year-old girls are apt to show a preference for gender-typed toys and materials. Three-year-olds' pretend play is frequently fixated on a particular prop, as with the baby doll. To extend their imaginative play, three-year-olds delight in using additional props, such as the baby's bottle or a soft blanket.

Three-year-olds have fun trying their hands at creating different characters and a variety of scenes in their imaginative play. But these often don't last very long, such as when Lisa converts from her caregiver role to become a chef. Three-year-olds find it quite easy to switch roles as they invent, then move on to their next play theme.

Over the weekend, Molly, Xavier, and Drew attended open house events at various local military bases where their parents serve. The three individually decide to re-create some of the special things that interested them. They use their imaginations to dramatize the activities at the manipulatives table using Lego bricks, Tinkertoys, and soldier figurines.

Four-year-old Drew says, "I need lots of soldiers to march on the parade ground." Then he asks Molly, an older three-year-old, "Can I have some of your Tinkertoys for my cannon?" He adds, "I'll give you some of my Lego blocks. Okay?" They decide to trade materials. When Drew finishes designing his parade-ground cannon, he enthusiastically bellows out lots of loud "boom-boom-boom" sounds.

Meanwhile, Molly uses the Lego bricks to build the large hospital where her mom trains to become an Army dentist. She says, "Thanks for the Lego blocks, Drew. Look how tall my hospital is now."

Xavier, a four-year-old, decides to construct a helicopter with Tinkertoys to look like the ones his dad maintains at his base. Holding the completed helicopter high, he flies it over the table and makes rapid "dat-dat-dat-dat" noises. Molly cautions, "Do not crash into my hospital."

Four-year-olds, and sometimes three-year-olds, engage in what is called *associative play*, where the preschoolers play separately from each other while being involved in shared interests, such as the open houses at the military bases. The children talk about the materials and their activities or behaviors. Although they are socializing during this stage of play development, their own individual play preferences are the most important to them.

Imitative imaginative play themes are frequently built around experiences preschoolers have had with their friends and families, or activities in the community. Four-year-olds, especially boys, are delighted with intense, loud, and noisy pretend play, such as Drew making a bold boom with his cannon and Xavier vocalizing the forceful whirring blades of his helicopter. When Xavier flew his noisy helicopter, this also added some complexity and depth to enhance his imaginative play.

Four-year-olds, like Drew, are beginning to use negotiation skills to help them solve their problems. And preschoolers are learning about the benefits of such a give-and-take strategy during play, as Molly did.

After a recent violent storm with howling winds, thunder and lightning, flooding rain, and power outages, several four-year-old boys determine that they should create a command central to handle frightening emergencies. Arifeen announces, "I'll be the commander," and puts on a police officer's hat from the dramatic play center. He begins to appoint roles, making Ben the fire chief and Swapnil the head of the emergency medical technicians. The boys discuss different ways to make walkie-talkies, so they can communicate with each other. Ben suggests, "Let's put round stickers for buttons on the wooden blocks. Then attach pipe cleaners as antennas." In case of a power loss, they will snatch the flashlights used for colored light dancing.

Then the boys have an emergency call come in. Commander Arifeen sends Fire Chief Ben to a burning car crash. He says urgently, "Go, go!" "Yes sir," replies Ben as he grabs his large, red plastic-block fire truck, applies the siren, and races to put out the fire. Arifeen directs Swapnil, "Send Max with the ambulance to the crash scene." Meanwhile, Swapnil puts on his white doctor's jacket and uses a marker to print a sign that reads "EMGC RM" to stick on the refrigerator-box hospital. The boys work together at the scene to put out the fire and to rescue the cars' drivers. The injured are rushed to the emergency room, sirens roaring on the large, yellow plastic-block ambulance.

During what is called *cooperative play*, four-year-olds incorporate ideas from others, such as how to create the walkie-talkie, as they share planning around a particular play theme. They learn to develop a plan, and then act on it. In this well-organized form of social play, as seen in the command-central scenario, defined roles within the group, such as the fire chief, are usually assigned by a leader of the group. In cooperative play, four-year-olds are interested in the people and the

activity. As Jamari, one of my preschoolers, explained, "We are not on teams, but we are working together!" While three-year-olds play best with a small group of three children, four-year-olds relate successfully to four or five children in a group.

Four-year-olds truly enjoy exciting, wild, imaginative play. For example, the boys playing command central are anticipating an emergency after experiencing the loud thunder and power outages. They concentrate on details during pretend play, such as planning together to place sticker-buttons on their walkie-talkies so they can communicate. Preschoolers creatively use their imaginations to envision various items as symbols for their play props, such as having the large, colored plastic blocks represent the emergency vehicles.

Props and accessories help enhance the imaginary play themes. A white shirt from the housekeeping center turns into a doctor's coat and adds realism. Easy availability of writing materials enables preschoolers, like the doctor, to create written props such as the emergency-room sign. When real props aren't available, preschoolers will find a solution together to create their own!

Imaginative play provides amazing opportunities for preschoolers to develop their leadership skills while enacting various roles, such as a firefighter or a doctor. They learn to give and follow directions. Pretending to be the "good" guy or the "bad" guy enables them to perceive the world through another's viewpoint as they explore various scenarios.

As three-year-olds are still trying to determine if things are make-believe or real during imaginative play, particularly if the activity is a bit scary, four-year-olds are enjoying developing roles that make them feel in control and powerful. Even though four-year-old play can be fanciful, children of this age have developed a good grasp of fantasy versus reality.

As they explore their feelings, a wonderful aspect of imaginative play is that it allows the players to build in a variety of safety nets and work through scary situations. For example, a real flashlight is available during the emergency theme in case of a power outage or a frightening dark night. Or the children might keep a stuffed-animal dog handy, so it could bark to protect the players from burglars!

Frequently, preschoolers become caught up in violent imaginative play with superheroes and bad guys. These themes can be influenced by TV shows, movies, and video games. This pretend play can be prompted by scripted words, such as *pow* and *bam*. Or it can be used as a springboard for children to develop their own imaginative dialogue as they make choices and share materials to rescue citizens during an earthquake or operate a space station.

What You Can Do

- **Don't rush imaginary play.** Give young children plenty of time to plan their theme. They may need to gather or create their special props. Preschoolers need lots of time to become involved and play out their theme before they move toward closure.
- **Offer accessories to represent daily life as well as community activities.** Place kitchen equipment and baby things in the dramatic play center. Be sure to include objects from different cultural backgrounds; you might stock assorted clothing (such as scarves or straw hats), food containers (perhaps boxes with labels in various languages), and utensils (maybe chopsticks or a pizza pan). Stimulate imaginative play about the neighborhood with toy dump trucks, uniforms, and community helper figurines.
- **Provide open-ended materials.** Encourage preschoolers to explore these items to extend their play. Use cardboard boxes to paint or tape together to become vehicles, castles, or machines. Offer damp sand for molding into a wedding cake or a giant dinosaur. Pieces of fabric can become a superhero cape or a picnic blanket. Play music for an ice skater's waltz or a rock-band concert.
- **Strategically place props.** Go crazy! Place puppets in the music center for a musical show or exciting dance routine. Add kitchen utensils (egg beaters, funnels, and basters) to the water table so that children can create such things as pretend hurricanes. Display a wild assortment of hats in the block area to influence imaginative construction ideas. Small

figurines (dinosaurs and farm animals) at the art table could signal interesting creative scenarios with clay volcanoes or man-eating pipe cleaner vines.

- **Inspire imaginative play outdoors.** It's a delightfully acceptable place to be noisy and run around! Climbing equipment could become a spaceship or magic kingdom. Provide a hose near the tricycles and you could have a car wash! If you add shovels to the sand pit, then pirates or archeologists could dig for exciting treasures. With sidewalk chalk, the preschoolers could draw roadways for toy cars and trucks. Children could act out the "Three Billy Goats Gruff" folk tale next to the slide.

Other Aspects to Consider—Alerts

- **Keep an eye on the reticent child.** You may notice a child who never interacts in imaginative play with the others or just watches from a distance. He may still be in the onlooker stage and not yet ready to participate in play. Or he may be naturally timid or shy. He may exhibit a slow-to-warm-up temperament. However, if he continues to always be in an isolated position, make sure he is not being ostracized by others. You may need to coach him about ways to enter play interactions.

- **A child may find it difficult to use her imagination.** You may observe a child who appears to be resistant to new ideas. She seems to be quite rigid and finds it hard to be creative. She may even find things that the other preschoolers think are fun or exciting to be stupid. One on one, try simple imaginative activities with her, such as rolling playdough balls and then asking, "What do you think we could we do with these?"

- **Notice if one child always has to be the leader.** Does he play cooperatively and share materials with his peers? Or does he act as a bully, always assigning roles and insisting that others follow his directions? If he is inclined to exclude some children from imaginative play groups, help him learn to make play suggestions that are more inclusive. He might need to work with a therapist if he bullies others, trying to control them in negative and hurtful ways.

Activities for Parents to Try at Home

- **Create a shadow show.** Find a white wall or hang up a light-colored sheet for a screen. Gather and turn on several flashlights and turn off the room lights to make it dark. Encourage your child to make shadow characters on the screen with her hands and body. Ask her to use her imagination. Does she see a bird? A flower? Together, you can develop an exciting dialogue for your shadow players.

- **Change things around.** After acting out your child's favorite stories, try giving them a little twist for fun. Maybe the Three Little Pigs could live in houses of plastic, glass, and snow. What would happen if Cinderella went to a water skiing competition instead of a ball? What if Grandma came to visit Little Red Riding Hood instead of the girl doing the traveling?

- **Expand play with open-ended questions.** Encourage your preschooler to really use her creative imagination with some of the following types of questions: "Where might the wolf go next?" "What would happen if the dragon spit honey instead of fire?" "How could you become invisible?" Also, sometimes this type of questioning can help slow down play that has become too wild.

- **Explore the world with travel props.** Invite your child to go wherever his imagination will take him—he might take short trips (to the fair or the beach) or long trips (to the jungle or Washington, DC). Provide old tickets, travel magazines, maps, postcards, a suitcase, a backpack, a camera, sunglasses, and a beach towel. Create a pretend bus, plane, car, or boat with chairs, boxes, and pillows. Bon voyage!

- **Investigate nature.** My son, Gregg, and I spent many hours in the garden letting our minds wander. Geranium petals became lovely stick-on red fingernails for me and bloody, creepy nails for him. Dried acorn tops were little brown puppet caps on top of our fingers. Pinched from behind, snap dragons are funny, tiny talking faces. We wove daisies into a circle for my queen's crown, while large green oak  leaves stuck together with their stems proclaimed Gregg the prince of the garden kingdom. No garden? Try the park or search through a flower bouquet for natural accessories.

RELATED BOOKS TO READ WITH CHILDREN

Johnson, Crockett. 1955/2015. *Harold and the Purple Crayon.* New York: HarperCollins.

McAllister, Angela. 2005. *Harry's Box.* New York: Bloomsbury.

McLerran, Alice. 2004. *Roxaboxen.* New York: HarperCollins.

Seuss, Dr. 1937/1989. *And to Think That I Saw It on Mulberry Street.* New York: Random House Books for Young Readers.

Shaw, Charles G. 1988. *It Looked Like Spilt Milk.* New York: HarperCollins.

Young, Ed. 2002. *Seven Blind Mice.* New York: Puffin Books.

11

MILESTONES IN
SOCIAL DEVELOPMENT

Now that we have explored various aspects of social development among three- and four-year-olds, you might want to review the important milestones children tend to reach during the preschool years. Although these characteristics are typical of many children this age, they are not necessarily true of all of them, nor do they always appear at the same times.

The examples you have seen in each chapter help you know what to look for, and the strategies help you be prepared to deal with challenges that arise in your classroom. With this knowledge, you can appreciate the progress you will see in preschoolers' social skills as they grow up in stages.

Skills	Three-Year-Olds	Four-Year-Olds
Friendships	• They easily move in and out of play with new friends when interests change. • They are attracted to friends because of proximity, interest in an activity, or appeal of an exciting skill.	• More cooperative, they find it exciting and fun to participate in collaborative small-group projects with friends. • Appearing inseparable, they often enjoy intense best-friend relationships with children of the same sex.
Sharing and cooperation	• Still egocentric, they do not yet feel it is okay for others to play with their personal possessions, especially without asking permission. • With practice and time, they eventually learn that sharing an item is temporary and it will be returned.	• They discover that it's exciting to share ideas, materials, and each other's company while cooperating on projects. • They learn to trade and begin to negotiate in attempts to solve sharing problems during cooperative play.
Happiness	• They feel elated when they persist and successfully accomplish a task. • Feelings of great joy are produced when special adults in their lives connect and play with them.	• If they gain recognition from their peers, they feel valued. • They really love having experiences with hands-on activities and playing with their friends.
Teasing	• They may be unsuccessful when attempting to initiate fun teasing because they do not really understand what makes it funny or effective. • They learn ways to tease and behave toward others by mimicking their teachers, parents, siblings, peers, and TV characters.	• They like to show off their power and gain attention with verbal teasing, often using inappropriate language; they bully others this way. • With their high energy levels, they enjoy nonverbal teasing activities, such as bumping shoulders, making funny faces, and playing tag.
Rough-and-tumble play	• They happily amuse themselves as they repeat simple, big body movements such as jumping, spinning, and dancing. • With friends, they enjoy imitating roughhousing activities, such as pillow fighting, that they do at home with their parents.	• Depending on the specific needs of the other participants (experience levels and disabilities, for example), they experiment with how to adjust their physical play interactions. • Participating in rough-and-tumble play activities, such as tag or tug-of-war, they learn how to play by the rules while interacting with others.

Social Development of Three- and Four-Year-Olds

Skills	Three-Year-Olds	Four-Year-Olds
Diversity	• They identify, label, and match others according to various characteristics that are sometimes connected to race (eye shape, hair texture, and skin color). • They often make generalizations, which may become stereotypical views of others.	• They are aware of names given by society for various racial groups. • They don't exactly understand the concept of culture, but they are aware of concrete differences in clothing, language, foods, and eating styles.
Gender awareness	• They are well aware of gender identity, that is, knowing whether they are boys or girls. • They demonstrate a preference for gender-typed play activities.	• They look at clothing accessories and physical appearance as ways to distinguish gender identity. • They are aware that anatomy differs between the sexes.
Listening	• They enjoy creating their own rhymes and silly sounds as they contrive to manipulate and change words. • They actively listen to and respond to two-part directions, including following directional commands.	• They love listening to others' silly jokes and riddles. • They enjoy showing off that they can successfully meet the challenge of completing a set of three-step directions.
Verbal communication	• They comfortably speak with three or four words in a sentence. • They enjoy asking questions that begin with *what, where, who, when,* and *how.*	• They clearly communicate with four or more words in a sentence. • They are becoming more skilled in initiating conversations and less likely to interrupt the current speaker.
Imaginative play	• In a form of parallel play, they sit next to other young three-year-olds as they enjoy playing with similar materials. • They like to mimic real-life experiences and re-create daily routines during pretend play.	• They engage in loosely organized types of associative play that involve playing separately from others, possibly including three-year-olds, while being involved in a shared interest. • When involved in cooperative play, a well-organized form of social play, defined roles are usually assigned by a group leader.

INDEX

A

active listening, defined, 52

active listening skills

activities for, 56–58

children's books related to, 58

and language development, 53, 54

milestones for, 75

and phonological awareness, 56

precautions, 57

typical behaviors, 52–56

anti-racism work, 1–2

anxiety, 20

associative play, 68

B

brain-derived neurotrophic factor (BDNF), 34

bullying, 11, 28, 30, 37, 71

See also teasing

C

children's books

for active listening skills, 58

for diversity awareness, 44

for friendships, 12

for gender awareness, 51

for happiness, 25

for imaginative play, 72

for rough-and-tumble play, 38

for sharing, 18

for teasing, 31

for verbal communication skills, 65

communication skills. See verbal communication skills

cooperation, 13

See also sharing

cooperative play, 15–16, 18, 69

cultural differences. See diversity awareness

D

diversity, defined, 39

diversity awareness

    activities for, 42–43

    children's books related to, 44

    milestones for, 75

    precautions, 43–44

    typical behaviors, 39–42

dual language learners, 64

F

friendships

    activities for, 10, 11–12

    children's books related to, 12

    defined, 6

    intergenerational, 9, 12

    milestones for, 74

    precautions, 10–11

    and problem-solving skills, 9

    typical behaviors, 6–9

G

gender awareness

    activities for, 49, 50–51

    children's books related to, 51

    defined, 45

    milestones for, 75

    and play, 46, 47, 48

    precautions, 50

    and stereotypes, 48–49, 51

    typical behaviors, 45–49

gross motor activities. See rough-and-tumble play

H

happiness

    activities for, 22–23, 24

    children's books related to, 25

    defined, 19

    milestones for, 74

    precautions, 23–24

    typical behaviors, 19–22

hearing impairments, 57

I

imaginative play

    activities for, 70–72

    children's books related to, 72

    defined, 66

    milestones for, 75

    precautions, 71

    typical behaviors, 66–70

    See also play

L

llanguage skills. See verbal communication skills

listening skills. See active listening skills

M

Manwell, Elizabeth, 1

media influences

    on gender stereotypes, 51

    and physical roughness, 38

    and teasing, 29

multiculturalism. See diversity

    awareness

P

parallel play, 67

Parten, Mildred, 67

pets, 12

phonological awareness, 56

play

    associative, 68

    cooperative, 69

    and gender awareness, 46, 47, 48

    imitative, 7, 67

    parallel, 67

    See also imaginative play; rough-

    and-tumble play

potty language, 28, 30

    See also language skills

praise, 23–24

problem-solving skills, 9

R

reading, and verbal communication

    skills, 60–61

responsibility, 22

rough-and-tumble play

    activities for, 36–38

    and brain growth, 34

    children's books related to, 38

    defined, 32

    milestones for, 74

    precautions, 37

    vs. rough play, 32

    typical behaviors, 32–36

    See also play

S

sharing

    activities for, 16–18

    children's books related to, 18

    defined, 13

    difficulties in, 7–8, 14

    milestones for, 74

    and negotiation, 16

    precautions, 17

    typical behaviors, 13–16

social development, milestones for,

    73–75

social rejection, 28

    See also teasing

T

teasing

    activities for, 29–30, 31

    children's books related to, 31

    defined, 26

    milestones for, 74

    positive vs. negative, 27

    and potty language, 28

    precautions, 30

    typical behaviors, 26–29

television. See media influences

V

verbal communication, defined, 59

verbal communication skills

    and active listening, 53, 54

    activities for, 63–65

    adult modeling of, 31

    children's books related to, 65

    inappropriate words, 28, 30

    milestones for, 75

    precautions, 64

    and reading to children, 60–61

    typical behaviors, 59–63

    See also active listening skills

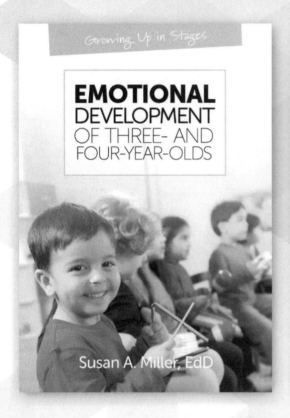